First published in 2004 by New Holland Publishers (UK) Ltd
London • Cape Town • Sydney • Auckland
Garfield House, 86–88 Edgware Road, London W2 2EA United Kingdom
www.newhollandpublishers.com
80 McKenzie Street, Cape Town 8001, South Africa
Level 1, Unit 4, 14 Aquatic Drive, Frenchs Forest, NSW 2086, Australia
218 Lake Road, Northcote, Auckland, New Zealand
Copyright © 2004 text AG&G Books
Copyright © 2004 illustrations and photographs New Holland Publishers (UK) Ltd
Copyright © 2004 New Holland Publishers (UK) Ltd

ISBN 1 84330 677 8
10 9 8 7 6 5 4 3 2 1

Editorial Direction: Rosemary Wilkinson Senior Editor: Clare Hubbard Production: Hazel Kirkman

Designed and created for New Holland by AG&G Books Copyright © 2004 "Specialist" AG&G Books
Design: Glyn Bridgewater Illustrations: Gill Bridgewater and Coral Mula Editor: Fiona Corbridge
Photographs: AG&G Books, Ian Parsons, Builder Center, Marshalls and Do It All

Reproduction by Pica Digital Pte Ltd, Singapore

Printed and bound in Malaysia by Times Offset (M) Sdn. Bhd.

Contents

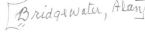

[Bridgewater, Alan]

Authors' foreword

What could be better, on a warm summer's day, than to relax on the patio with family and friends. A patio gives you somewhere pleasant to read a book, talk quietly, play with the children, cook on the barbecue, watch a water feature, and go to sleep on a lounger—all wonderfully therapeutic, quality-time experiences that everyone should enjoy. And then when the sun goes down in the evening, you can switch on some soft lights and music, and invite neighbors round for a party. Have you ever noticed that when people are on a patio, away from the confines of the house and the formalities observed in indoor spaces, they are generally more relaxed and expansive? They smile and laugh, make bigger movements with their hands, stride around and tend to behave in a less inhibited way. It is almost as if the great outdoors is our natural habitat—perhaps it is!

So there you have it—this is the age of the garden room. No more hiding away indoors: now is the time to build the biggest and best room in the house—the patio. This book will guide you through all the stages of designing, planning, and building. Now is the time to turn your patio dreams into patio reality.

Measurements

This book uses metric measurements. To convert these to imperial measurements, multiply the figure given in the text by the relevant number shown in the table below. Conversions are approximate.

To convert	Multiply by
inches to millimeters	25.4
feet to meters	0.3048
yards to meters	0.9144
sq. inches to sq. millimeters	645.16
sq. feet to sq. meters	0.092903
sq. yards to sq. meters	0.83612
cu. feet to cu. meters	0.02831
cu yards to cu. meters	0.7646
pounds to grams	453.592
pounds to kilograms	0.4536
gallons to litres	4.545

Assessing your garden

Asuccessful patio relies on achieving a balance between your requirements and the character of the garden. Almost every garden is big enough for a patio, and even in the tiniest yard, you can go a long way to modeling the space to make a comfortable "room" open to the sky. The first step is to spend time in your garden, deciding what you require from a patio. Look at the space, talk through how you want to use it, and then make plans to fulfil these aims.

Will my garden be big enough? How do I start?

MAKING PLANS

When you have looked long and hard at your garden, assessed its size and character, and decided on the scope and style of the patio, work out how to set the whole plan in action.

Let's say that your garden is on a slope and you want to build a brick patio close to the house. Are you going to bring in material to level out the slope and create a flat area for the patio? Or are you going to move the existing earth around to make a terraced area? Will new ground levels mean that you have to adjust the height of your fences? If the new patio means you will be sitting at a higher level, will this impact upon your privacy or that of your neighbors? Do you have to consider the position of existing drains, or build drains to take water away from the patio? Think about all the implications of going ahead with the project, and ways to deal with them.

GARDEN SIZE

Take the size and shape of your garden, your needs, and budget into account, and plan out the patio.

Decide how much space you are prepared to relinquish to the patio. If you are preparing for retirement, you might opt for a large, low-maintenance patio with easy-to-manage raised beds. If you have young children, your priority might be a safe, enclosed space for them to play in. If you delight in eating outdoors, you might prefer a patio close to the house. If you are aiming for a retreat where you can read, a private space well away from the house might appeal.

A diminutive courtyard garden that has been leveled and paved with pale, light-reflecting tiles. Metal containers help to bounce light and also glint attractively. A narrow strip of earth has been kept as a border.

GARDEN STYLE

Tucked away in a walled garden, bricks and cobblestones are used to draw a bold semicircle.

Just like the rooms in your home, the style of the patio should be planned to suit your lifestyle and needs. However, the choice you make will to a great extent be dictated by the form and age of your house, the shape and size of your garden, and, of course, your own particular likes and dislikes.

If you want privacy, it doesn't make much sense to build raised decking that puts you in full view of your neighbors. If you have teenage children, a barbecue might be a popular feature. If you enjoy sleeping outdoors, a patio with low lights, a covered area, and bunk beds would be great fun. If you have always fancied a hammock, incorporate a couple of posts into your patio. Decide how much time you want to dedicate to construction, think about possible materials (stone, brick, concrete, or wood) and then choose a style that will look good in the established surroundings.

A decking patio with seaside overtones—matching raised beds are topped with decorative turquoise crushed stone.

Choosing a patio, path, and steps

What will be the best option for my garden?

There are hundreds of ways to make a patio, and many materials to choose from. A stone patio could be made of real cut stone slabs, reconstituted stone slabs, cleft stone, crushed stone, stone set on edge, or stone plus brick. There are also brick patios, wooden decking patios, and patios made from gravel, bark, or sawdust. Alongside your patio you may need paths and steps. Whatever the size of your garden, there will be an exciting option for you.

TYPES OF PATIO

Basic patio
Plain and functional

→ The specifications of a basic patio are that it is a simple shape, with little detailing. It might consist of an area of plain cast concrete, or be made up of plain concrete slabs, gravel, brick, or even bark. However, the shape will be rectilinear, and there will be no changes of level or decorative edgings. For any patio, the expense and expertise involved depend on the amount of detail in the design, so a basic patio is both inexpensive and relatively easy to build. (See page 24.)

Decorative patio
Patterned and detailed

↗ A decorative patio is both functional and visually dynamic. The design attempts to use materials in a stimulating way. Plain stone blocks are exciting in their own right, but set alongside cobblestones, they can create magic! (See page 36.)

Decking patio
The beauty of wood

↗ Decking can be made of anything from planks of rough-sawn lumber to wood that has been planed, molded, and pressure-treated with preservatives. (See page 34.)

Avoiding slippery surfaces

In Europe, wood sold specifically as "decking" is generally grooved on the upper surface. These grooves help to provide a good footing in damp weather conditions.

OTHER PATIO OPTIONS

Natural patio ~ This is a patio that imitates nature. If we define a patio as a dry, level area that is fairly comfortable underfoot, a natural patio could therefore be made from shingle or sand to resemble a beach, from pine needles to reflect a forest floor, from shale to mimic a mountainside, or from long grass to look like a meadow. (See page 30.)

Salvaged mixed-media patio ~ A patio made from a mixture of salvaged materials such as old tiles and bricks, railroad ties, sawdust, or tree slices—any safe, salvaged materials that can be put down to make a level area.

Raised or sunken patio ~ Patios that are set either above or below ground level. An old, unused swimming pool can be covered over and turned into a wonderful patio by installing heating, bubbling fountains, and exotic plants. (See page 38.)

High-tech patio ~ A patio that uses modern materials such as stainless steel, copper sheet, or glass bricks to create a surface that draws inspiration from industrial materials.

DECORATIVE PAVERS

You must consider cost, suitability, and ease of handling. Bricks are expensive, but fairly light in weight. Reconstituted stone slabs are cheaper, but very heavy. Purpose-designed pavers (super-hard, thin concrete or clay bricks) offer another possibility. Think about the decorative potential of various materials, work out how you will lift the individual units, then make your choice.

Bricks are the perfect option for a traditional country cottage garden.

Modern reconstituted stone slabs are both functional and decorative.

A design of bricks combined with pavers can look really striking.

Cleft-stone paving is made from small pieces of stone.

A selection of different types of real stone makes an unusual patio.

Decking tile paths can easily be constructed from readily available wood.

TYPES OF STEPS

Brick and stone steps
A traditional option for a cottage garden

← Brick and stone steps are a favored choice because not only are the materials reasonably low in cost and easy to handle, but the design possibilities are endless. A good, easy-to-build option for steps is to use bricks for the risers and side walls, and cleft-stone paving for the treads.

Wooden steps
Inexpensive and easy to construct

A wide, low fight of steps with railroad tie risers and stone shingle treads.

Slow-rise decking steps leading to a decking patio—good for a sloping site.

PATIO ADDITIONS

When the patio is finished, you can start to consider additional features and furnishings for it. Think of the patio as a garden room, just like a room in your house, to which you can add various items to make it more comfortable, user-friendly, or attractive.

Depending upon the climate in your area and the situation of your house, you might need shelter from the wind, and an arbor with a plant canopy to keep off the sun. Will you be using the patio at night? If so, you may need lighting or heating. Which family requirements do you need to cater for? Perhaps you'd like a barbecue, a large table for family meals, a sand corner for the toddlers, or a bed for the dog. Do you want storage space? You might fancy erecting a hammock—will you need to put in posts to hang it from?

Do you want planters or raised beds for plants, or a small herb garden? Do you want to incorporate a gently trickling water feature? Live in the new garden room for several weeks before you make any hard and fast decisions.

A raised bed made from reconstituted stone makes a beautiful addition to a reconstituted stone slab patio.

A traditional Japanese feature—water gently dribbling into a stone basin—would enhance a natural patio.

Checking the site

*What do I
need to look
out for on
the site?*

Before you start work, check the site to make sure that there aren't any practical factors that are going to cause difficulties. You need to consider everything, from the position of underground pipes to overhead cables, the way the sun affects the site at different times of day, shadows cast by trees, where a power supply will run from—anything that might cause trouble. Draw up a hit-list of potential problems and make sure that they aren't going to hold you back.

SITE CHECKLIST

Stand on the proposed site and look slowly around you. Look at the house, the trees, and the position of the sun. Assess the degree to which the patio is overlooked by adjoining houses.

Sun and shade ~ Study the position of the sun at times when you are likely to use the patio. You will probably want to avoid heavy shade, and you need to think about how to deal with full sun—it might be too strong to sit in, so you may wish to counter it by providing a shaded area, such as under an arbor, or buy garden furniture to do the job.

Scale, orientation, and viewpoints ~ Walk around the garden in order to view the site from a good number of positions. Do you want to see the patio from indoors? Do you want it to be an open, public space or a secluded spot, on high or low ground?

Providing shelter ~ Most patios need shelter—from the sun and wind, for privacy, and for planting. If you live in an unpredictable climate, a covered area to provide shelter from light showers might be a good idea.

Problems above and below ground ~ Avoid a site that is crossed by underground supply lines for utilities. If there are overhanging trees, will they drip on you? Keep away from tree roots, because they might cause concrete to crack.

Soil type and digging ~ Dig a few test holes to check whether or not it is possible to build on that site. If there are old concrete footings, an old pond, wet areas, or pockets of sand, these may cause difficulties and the design of the patio may have to be modified accordingly. A site on wet clay will be a lot of hard work to dig, so you may prefer to choose a site that requires less digging.

PRESERVING PRECIOUS TOPSOIL

If you are going to move a lot of soil or lay down a concrete slab, you have to avoid burying the fertile topsoil, which is the layer plants need to grow. As you strip away the topsoil, put it to one side. Shovel the sterile subsoil onto an area that needs to be built up. Finally, bring the topsoil back to the site and spread it over the subsoil.

GROUND CONDITIONS AND PROBLEMS

If the ground in the proposed site is overly boggy, sandy, or rocky, there is a risk that the conditions will in some way be a nuisance—either while the work is in progress or when the patio has been completed. It is usually possible to overcome these problems, but sometimes it is simpler to opt for another location, or to build a raised patio that doesn't require digging.

THINGS TO CONSIDER BEFORE STARTING TO BUILD A PATIO

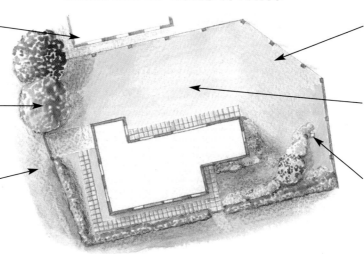

Overlooking buildings
Avoid siting a patio in full view of neighboring houses, unless you want to be an exhibit.

Overhanging trees
Too many overhanging trees can be a problem—dripping after rain, dropping sticky fruit, etc.

Proximity to a road
If the road is very busy, avoid noise and fumes by building the patio on the other side of the garden.

Degree of exposure
It is good to have a view, but is the site too breezy, or exposed to driving rain?

Shade
Most people like a patio to have plenty of sun, but is there enough shade?

Septic tank
If your property has a septic tank, build the patio well away from it to avoid the nuisance of odor, flies, or overflow.

Designing a project

Once you have decided on the type of patio—size, style, and location—it is most important to draw out a plan and make design notes on paper. When all the facts are set out, you will be able to do calculations to work out quantities of materials required. This written record of specifications will always be ready to refer to throughout the project—useful when contacting suppliers, and essential during the construction process.

Do I really need to draw designs?

Inspirations

Get yourself a folder complete with plain and gridded paper, pencils, a ruler, and colored crayons. Make a "wish list" of things you would like to have. If the design includes brick and stone, decide on colors and textures. Don't be too specific at this stage, just try to visualize the overall shape, color, and form. Start a scrapbook of pictures that inspire you (do not limit the collection: include everything at this stage).

YOUR CONCEPT

You may know that you want to build a patio by the house rather than a patio at the end of the garden, but are you aware of the available materials, colors, and textures? Talk the idea over with your family and friends, perhaps even with your neighbors.

VISUALIZING

Cover the ground with something the same size as the envisaged patio, such as a tarpaulin. Live with this full-size plan for a few days and see how it impacts on your use of the garden. Could it be bigger? Does it need to be realigned? Set out tables and chairs and try it out—does it feel right?

DESIGN CONSIDERATIONS

Look closely at your chosen materials in order to balance their dimensions with the proposed structure. If, for example, you are building a rectangular brick patio, the starting point for the design will be the surface pattern you would like, and the width and length of the patio in terms of whole bricks. It is much better to spend extra time at the design stage to avoid problems later.

DRAWING YOUR DESIGN

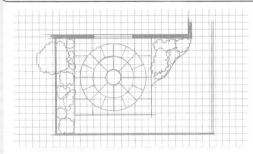

↗ *Use gridded paper to ensure an accurate plan, which will help you assess how the proposed position of the patio will relate to the house and garden.*

Measure your garden and draw the plan to scale on gridded paper, so that each square is a set measurement. Draw the patio on the plan so that its position is distanced from a couple of fixed points, such as the house and a boundary fence. If you are building a structure from manufactured materials (bricks, slabs, or blocks), draw out the various views. As far as possible, size the structure to use whole units, and minimize complex cutting.

PLANTING CONSIDERATIONS

If you plan to have a patio with a vine-covered arbor, raised beds, and various pockets of planting, you cannot build the patio and then backtrack in order to remove parts of the structure and accommodate these desires—the position of planting areas must be established at design stage.

Decide on planting areas and map them on paper. When you are marking out the patio site on the ground, set out the planting areas and put a frame around them. Make sure that they are kept free of hardpan and concrete during the construction process.

Checklist

• Is the design suited to the size and character of your garden?

• Have you worked out the exact dimensions?

• Do these need to relate to unit sizes?

• Have you chosen the best materials at the lowest cost?

• Is the design structurally sound?

• Do you know how it is constructed?

• Is the patio going to interfere with the integrity of existing structures?

FOOTINGS

If you are using brick, stone, or blocks, you will first need to build a stable footing under the structure. This will ensure that the structure resists summer and winter ground movement and stays in one piece.

Designing with brick

Good brickwork means designing a structure that minimizes the need to cut bricks; also the vertical joints should be offset in neighboring courses. In most instances, manufactured items such as preformed concrete slabs and blocks are compatible with whole brick sizes.

Important principles

Are there any set rules or principles to follow?

The principles that govern the shape of a space, and dictate the character and size of its contents in relation to that space, have gradually evolved over time to produce a set of rules that we know from experience give exciting, well-balanced results, so it is best to adhere to them. Read through the guiding principles described below, and see how they relate to your proposed patio and any other garden structures that are planned.

House and garden

On paper, you might like the idea of symmetry—perhaps a patio centered on the house, with steps centered on the patio—however, you need to consider how this arrangement would affect your use of the patio.

Look at the relationship between the house, garden, and patio, decide how you want the elements to come together, and then start thinking about style. Never let form dominate function to the exclusion of everything else.

Doorway into house

Location, orientation, sun, shade, and wind

The three most important guiding rules are: location, location, location. Shape, color, texture, and design can be changed, but if the location is wrong, everything will feel wrong.

Go into the garden and conduct your own trials. Set out chairs, a table, and perhaps an old rug or two, and then over a two- or three-day period, try and get the feel of the location. Is there enough light? Is it a bit drafty? Does the wind whip between the house and a wall to funnel onto the patio? Is there enough dappled shade? If you enjoy sunbathing, can you do it in comfort and sufficient privacy?

Scale and critical measurements

The overall size of the patio, and the size and scale of the units that make it, need to be considered first separately and then together. You might decide that a good size for the patio is 25 feet long and 6 feet wide, but how does this equate to the size of your chosen units? The best plan is to adjust the size of a patio to fit your units. If you plan to use railroad ties, it is much easier to change the size of the patio, rather than cutting the sleepers.

Drainage slopes, damp courses, and air bricks

There is nothing quite as miserable as going out onto a patio after a shower and finding water hanging about in puddles and damp spots. Patios must be constructed with a very slight slope in order for water to drain off.

If a site is damp, walls need a damp course (felt at the bottom and tiles at the top). A raised patio with cavities underneath must have an air brick for ventilation.

Esthetics

The dictionary definition of "esthetics" is "pertaining to pure beauty rather than any other consideration; artistic or relating to good taste." While it is not easy to decide precisely what is and what isn't good taste, most of us intuitively enjoy some forms and shapes more than others. For example, in patio construction broad curves are usually more acceptable than jagged angles. It is just a matter of fashion whether or not one type of patio surface is thought to be esthetically pleasing at a particular moment and another is plain vulgar. If you lack confidence, look in books and magazines, ask friends, and draw all this information together to make your designs.

Practicality and feasibility

You might want a patio half the size of the garden, with a partially covered arbor to span it, but you need to balance what is practical against what is feasible. From a practical viewpoint everything might be fine—the levels are right, it doesn't obstruct your view from the house, and your neighbors are happy—but is it feasible? Does it comply with zoning regulations? Will the covered arbor make it difficult for you to maintain the house gutters? Will the arbor posts need footings? Can you afford the cost?

Look at the options, draw up your wish list, assess the costs, and then make a decision.

Sensible layout

Will a large patio impact upon your use of the garden? If the patio is a certain shape and size, will it inhibit access to a gate, or make it difficult to mow the lawn? Will its position block a favorite walk around the garden, or affect the route of paths?

Curves, circles, and straight lines

Beautiful sweeping curves excite the senses and draw the eye, but straight lines are easier to build than curved ones. The trick is to get a balance between what you would like, and what is possible on the ground.

The options for creating circles are many and varied. For example, you might find curved pavers, or you could just scribe out a circle and fill it with gravel, bark, or concrete. It is not easy to build a circular patio that consists entirely of bricks, because it will involve a lot of cutting; however, a brick edging is simple to achieve.

If you want to build a raised patio made from railroad ties, it is best to stay away from circles and curves and go for big, bold, straight lines.

Just as straight lines need to be straight—with no wobbles or curious deviations—so circles and curves need to be just right. Design-wise, broad, sweeping curves are less tense than little tight ones. From a practical viewpoint, it's easier to run the lawnmower around a broad curve than a small one. Curves made from part-circles are the easiest to construct.

Planning and preparation

What will I need? How long will it take?

Now is the time for drawing up lists, working out quantities, scheduling when you are going to do the work, deciding whether or not you need help with the heavier tasks, and calling around for prices and delivery times. If you put in time at the planning stage working out the fine details—from how much it is going to cost, to where the delivery men are going to put materials, and what happens if it's raining—the project should run in a orderly fashion!

SORTING OUT THE ORDER OF WORK

Each project needs to be planned out according to your particular situation, which is governed by the time of year, the size of your garden, who is helping, and so on. Your initial task is to decide on the order of work—what goes where, and when, and how.

Let's say that you are going to build a large patio of stone pavers. The basic order of work is to dig out the area for the footing, put down hardpan and beat it flat, spread sharp sand and compact it with a roller or power tamper, and lay the pavers.

You need to decide in advance where all the excavated earth is going, and where you are going to put the hardpan and sand. You don't want them spread out all over the place—you need a clear passage around the garden, and you don't want the materials getting damaged, or posing a safety hazard to children. It's important to plan out each stage and figure out the implications of the procedures in order to avoid unexpected headaches when you start work.

Order for building a paver patio
with stone pavers over sand

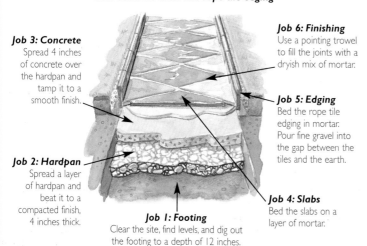

Job 5: Finishing
Replace and repair the lawn with turf or grass seed.

Job 4: Joints
Trickle silver sand into the joints—as much as they will take.

Job 3: Frame
Starting with the outer frame, set the pavers on blobs of cement. Lay the central motif.

Job 2: Sharp sand
Put 4 inches of sharp sand over the hardpan and compact it with a roller or power tamper.

Job 1: Footing
Dig out the footing to a depth of 10 inches, level the site, and put in 6 inches of compacted hardpan.

Order for building a decorative path
with concrete slabs and rope tile edging

Job 3: Concrete
Spread 4 inches of concrete over the hardpan and tamp it to a smooth finish.

Job 2: Hardpan
Spread a layer of hardpan and beat it to a compacted finish, 4 inches thick.

Job 1: Footing
Clear the site, find levels, and dig out the footing to a depth of 12 inches.

Job 6: Finishing
Use a pointing trowel to fill the joints with a dryish mix of mortar.

Job 5: Edging
Bed the rope tile edging in mortar. Pour fine gravel into the gap between the tiles and the earth.

Job 4: Slabs
Bed the slabs on a layer of mortar.

Have you got enough time and energy?

Balance the time available against your energy level. If you are fit, with plenty of time on your hands, you can spread the tasks over weeks instead of days. But if you are short of time, you will need to speed up the procedures. Assuming that you already have good tools, one or more wheelbarrows, and plenty of buckets, the biggest single timesaver you can invest in is a cement mixer.

TOOLS AND MATERIALS

Although the choice of materials will depend upon the project, there are two guiding principles: it is always best to use the correct tools for the task, and it is always less expensive to purchase materials in bulk. It may be tempting to use a spade to shift sand rather than buying a new shovel, but it will take you twice as long, and your back will suffer. And don't fall for buying your sand in one prepacked bag at a time—it will be very expensive!

GETTING QUOTES

You can cut costs by asking for quotes from local companies. List precisely what you want—name of product, size, color, and quantity—then call around for the best price. Never buy materials without seeing them: once you have the quotes, visit the suppliers and look at the products on offer. Having agreed on the price and the delivery date, it is preferable to pay only on delivery of the materials.

VACATIONS

Make sure that your schedule takes vacations into account. If you plan to work on a national holiday or on a summer weekend, you must order the materials well ahead. You cannot expect companies to deliver at such times or during unsocial hours.

TIMETABLE

If you are short of time, or asking friends to help (or paying for help), you must draw up a timetable. List the procedures and your expectations, and try to stick to completing the tasks in the allotted time. Build in some contingency time in case the weather turns ugly or there are other problems.

Delivery problems

Always assume that deliveries might be late and order your materials well in advance. If you are ordering in bulk, can the truck park outside your gate? Are you allowed to unload materials on the land in front of your house, or will it pose a hazard? If a crane will be used to winch jumbo bags of sand or pallets of bricks off the truck, is there a convenient spot where they can be lifted over your fence?

CALCULATING MATERIAL QUANTITIES

It is relatively easy to work out how many bricks you need for a particular job (see page 32), but not quite so simple to decide on quantities for sand, cement, and hardpan. Order sand in bulk, because it is cheaper that way, and if any is left over, use it elsewhere in the garden. Cement is both expensive and short-lived, so order only a few bags at a time.

➔ *Work out quantities, add on a little extra for good measure, and call at least three suppliers to check prices.*

40 high-fired, exterior-grade bricks per yard run of path

Wood 4 inches wide, 2 inches thick, length to suit

2 tons clean hardpan per 80-foot run of path

2 tons clean ballast per 80-foot run of path

1 ton soft sand per 80-foot run of path

Guidelines for calculating material quantities

Depending on the product, you need to work out the dimensions, the number of pieces, and/or the weight. Calculate the best number-to-price deal.

Hardpan ~ Usually sold by the truck-load. Work out how much you need, order the amount to the nearest whole load above that amount, and then dig the footings deeper to use up the extra.

Gravel and sand ~ A whole truck-load or jumbo bag is the cheapest option. Gift any left over to a neighbor.

Concrete ~ It's very difficult to work out how much you need. It is usually best to buy it one or two bags at a time, as and when it is needed.

Bricks and blocks ~ Bricks and concrete blocks are usually sold by the pallet-load. Buy a complete load and plan to use the surplus on another project. Brick seconds are sometimes a very good option, and much cheaper than standard quality. Over-fired seconds are particularly good. They tend to be misshapen, sometimes with corners missing, and generally look old and well worn. Their exciting colors and textures look wonderful in the garden.

WILL YOU NEED SOME HELP?

Building patios can be really good fun. If a friend or relative wants to help, why not agree? You will be giving the helper pleasure and spreading the workload. Digging footing holes and moving bricks is hard work. Are you fit enough for the tasks ahead? Do you think that you can take a week of bending, lifting, digging, and generally slogging it out with buckets and spades? If you have any doubts at all, check with a physician. The two biggest energy savers are a wheelbarrow and a power cement mixer, which are worth their weight in gold.

PROTECTING THE SURROUNDING AREA

If you are shifting earth and moving wheelbarrows over the lawn, it's a good idea to protect the grass with a plastic sheet or large sheets of plywood. If you are using a cement mixer, make sure that it is kept well away from the lawn and flowerbeds. Cement is very corrosive: it will damage skin and kill plants, so be careful how you use it. When doing repetitive tasks, such as walking from the cement mixer to the site, or using a wheelbarrow, try to vary the route, to avoid compacting the ground.

Tools and materials

Where do the tools and materials come from?

Tools and materials come from four main sources: home improvement centers for tools, builders' yards for bricks, pavers and tiles, dedicated local suppliers for bulk items such as sand and gravel, and garden centers for fixtures and fittings such as pots, lights, and water features. It is possible to make savings—in money by purchasing materials in bulk, in time by using the correct tools for the job, and in effort by buying the best tools that you can afford.

GENERAL CONSTRUCTION TOOLS AND MACHINERY

Tools for measuring and marking

Pegs and string

Small tape measure

Carpenter's level

Big tape measure

Tools for moving materials

Gloves

Wheelbarrow

Bucket

Tools for digging, compacting, mixing, and raking

Spade

Shovel

Fork

Sledgehammer

Garden rake

Trowel

Tools for brick, stone, concrete, and mortar

Stonemason's hammer

Mason's trowel

Brick hammer

Grinder

Brick chisel

Pointing trowel

Cold chisel

Miscellaneous tools

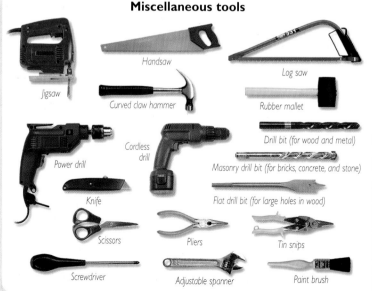

Handsaw

Log saw

Jigsaw

Curved claw hammer

Rubber mallet

Power drill

Cordless drill

Drill bit (for wood and metal)

Masonry drill bit (for bricks, concrete, and stone)

Knife

Flat drill bit (for large holes in wood)

Scissors

Pliers

Tin snips

Screwdriver

Adjustable spanner

Paint brush

Machinery and power tool safety

Always follow the manufacturer's directions. Never use power tools if you are exhausted or taking medication. If the weather is wet or the lawn covered in dew, make sure that you use the tools in conjunction with a GFCI (Ground Fault Circuit Interruptor). Keep children out of harm's way.

RENTING TOOLS

If you are going to put down a concrete footing under a structure, you can easily cut time and effort in half by renting a power tamper to thump the hardpan into place. (This machine is also used for firming paving materials into place.) Mixing mortar and concrete by hand is a chore, but a cement mixer makes the task easy and enjoyable.

GENERAL CONSTRUCTION MATERIALS

Brick and stone

Concrete paver

Artificial stone paver

Real stone paver

Flat stone

Radius paver

Artificial terra-cotta tile

Imitation stacked tiles (paver)

Building stone

Brick

Artificial stone block

Edging and corner post

Imitation stone blocks

Concrete paving block

Roof tile

Border tile

Slate

Cobblestones

Decorative gravel

Wood

Useful lumber sections

Rustic post

Log roll

Railroad tie

Log end

Post finial

Trellis

Bark chippings

Fixing materials

Zinc-plated screw

Zinc-plated carriage screw

Galvanized nail

Zinc-plated carriage bolt, washer, and nut

Materials for patio water features

Plastic sump

Rigid liner

Synthetic padding

Butyl liner (thick rubber)

Hosepipe

Armored pipe

Flexible plastic pipe

Flexible copper pipe

RECLAIMED MATERIALS

Professionally reclaimed materials like bricks and lumber are nearly always a good option in terms of quality and texture, but they can be expensive. While you can reduce the cost of professionally reclaimed materials by doing all the fetching and carrying yourself, a better option is to search out a small building that has been pulled down, and to do everything yourself—from sorting and selection through to . And, if you have friends or family with a pick-up truck, and they are willing to join in the fun, then so much the better!

CONCRETE AND MORTAR RECIPES

There are as many "best" recipes as there are builders. Do not use too much water, always use fresh Portland cement and hydrated lime, avoid using too much cement in the mortar, and use only clean, well-washed sand.

Cement Soft sand Sharp sand Gravel Ballast Lime

Concrete
For footings (and occasionally pond lining)

For general footings for block and brick walls

Cement + Sharp sand + Gravel

As above (this recipe uses ballast—a mixture of sand and gravel)

Cement + Ballast

For paths and light-duty footings

Cement + Ballast

Mortar
For building with bricks, blocks, and stone

For bricks and blocks, and general work

Cement + Soft sand

A special soft, smooth mortar for stonework

Cement + Lime + Soft sand

A special rough-textured mortar for wide courses in brick/stonework

Cement + Lime + Sharp sand

CAUTION

Cement and lime powder, wet concrete, and mortar are all corrosive!

Wear goggles, a mask, and gloves when mixing. If it is a hot or slightly breezy day, you must wash your face after mixing. Wear gloves while building with concrete and mortar.

Setting out the site

I lack confidence— will I be up to the task?

There is only one way to find out if you are equal to the challenge of building a patio, and that is to roll up your sleeves and get started. Measuring, digging, mixing concrete, counting bricks, sawing wood, and nailing boards together are all perennial features of the projects, and are within the capabilities of most people. Suppliers are generally happy to offer advice if you are unsure about a process. Make a good start by setting out the site with care.

POINTS TO CONSIDER

- Is your site dry and sandy, hard and rocky, or wet and squashy? You need to dig a trial hole to find out.
- If the ground is very sandy, you must either resite the project or dig much deeper footings that use a greater thickness of hardpan and concrete.
- If the ground is rocky you might not need (or be able) to lay a footing.
- If the ground is waterlogged, you must either resite the project, or lay pipes underneath the footings to drain off the excess water.
- If, when you are digging, you come across an unexpected pipe or cable (it might be electricity, water, gas, sewage, oil, or land drains), you must stop work and check it out.

CROSS-SECTIONS

A cross-section is a vertical slice through a project, right down to the footing. Draw a cross-section to help you to visualize how components fit together.

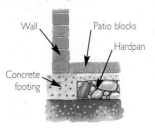

Wall

Patio blocks

Hardpan

Concrete footing

1. Check your measurements ~ You must measure the thickness of the various materials—for example, bricks, mortar courses, footings—so that you know how deep to dig the hole.

2. Draw to scale ~ Draw cross-sections to scale so that you have a clear understanding of the various layers and the order of work.

MARKING OUT SHAPES

Rectangular shapes

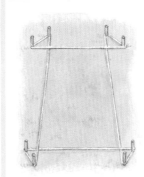

← Bang in a wooden peg to establish the position of one corner. Tie string to the peg and stretch it taut to set out one side. Turn off at a right angle to set out the next side, and so on until you have four sides marked out with pegs and string. To check the dimensions, measure diagonally from corner to corner and make small adjustments until these measurements are identical—at which time all the corners will be at right angles, and opposite sides will be equal.

Circles

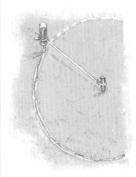

← Let's say that you want a circle 20 feet in diameter. Bang a wooden peg into the ground at the point where you imagine the center will be. Cut 21 feet of string and tie a loop at each end so that the string is 10 feet long when stretched taut. Slide one loop over the peg and walk around in a circle. When you are happy with the position of the circumference of the circle, slide a long-necked bottle, full of sand, into the other loop and scribe out the circle.

Curves

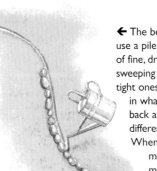

← The best way of marking out a free curve is to use a pile of cobblestones and a watering can full of fine, dry sand. Remembering that broad, sweeping curves are easier on the eye than small, tight ones, set out the cobblestones on the ground in what you consider is a good curve. Stand back and see if it looks right. Inspect it from different directions, and live with it for a while. When you are happy with the curve you have made (and this might take some time), mark the line with a generous trail of sand and remove the cobblestones.

Removing turf

Use a tape measure, pegs, and string to mark out the area on the ground. Take a spade and slice up the area into a spade-width grid. Hold the spade at a low angle and slice under the turf to remove one square. Repeat across the whole area.

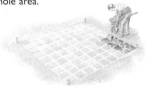

LEVELS

To create a level area on the ground, start by banging in a peg at the lowest point. Run a string to the higher ground and bang in another peg. Bridge the two pegs with a length of wood and check with a carpenter's level. Repeatedly lower the ground along the line of the string, tapping in the second peg until both pegs and ground are at the same level. Work out from these two points with additional pegs. Check the depth of a hole with a tape measure.

DEALING WITH SLOPES

If your ground is sloping, you have three choices. You can bring in materials to build up the slope to make a level plateau; dig into the slope and move the existing soil from the higher point to the lower point to create a level terrace; or give digging and earth-moving a miss, and build a raised decking patio that hovers over the sloping ground.

Much depends on the degree of slope, but for a gently sloping garden, the cheapest option is to define the edge of the patio with a brick retaining wall, and then move the earth within the enclosure until you achieve a level surface.

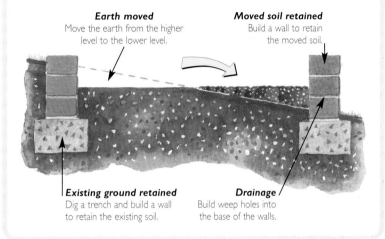

Earth moved
Move the earth from the higher level to the lower level.

Moved soil retained
Build a wall to retain the moved soil.

Existing ground retained
Dig a trench and build a wall to retain the existing soil.

Drainage
Build weep holes into the base of the walls.

DISPOSING OF EARTH

Digging holes creates waste earth. Topsoil is too precious to throw away and can always be put to good use somewhere in the garden. Subsoil, which is sterile, can be employed at the base of a decorative bank, rockery, or raised bed, or to fill in a boggy area at the edge of a pond, or banked around the edge of the patio. Try and plan the whole disposal exercise so that the earth only gets moved once, from the hole to its final destination in the garden.

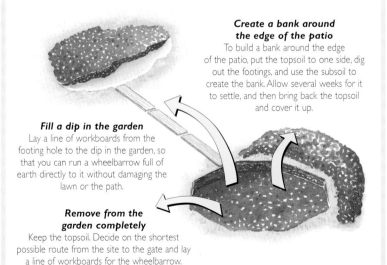

Create a bank around the edge of the patio
To build a bank around the edge of the patio, put the topsoil to one side, dig out the footings, and use the subsoil to create the bank. Allow several weeks for it to settle, and then bring back the topsoil and cover it up.

Fill a dip in the garden
Lay a line of workboards from the footing hole to the dip in the garden, so that you can run a wheelbarrow full of earth directly to it without damaging the lawn or the path.

Remove from the garden completely
Keep the topsoil. Decide on the shortest possible route from the site to the gate and lay a line of workboards for the wheelbarrow.

DIGGERS

One way to help with excavation is to rent a small digger. It will get the task done fast, but will your gates be wide enough? Will a digger compact the lawn and scrape the drive? Will it be able to maneuver without damaging borders, trees, and other features? If the patio is small, it is probably easier to ask friends to help and dig it by hand. If digging by hand is simply not an option, you have the choice of renting a digger and getting down to the task yourself, or renting a digger plus driver.

FORMWORK

The sides of a footing hole need to be stabilized. If the ground is hard, it is not necessary to do anything, but if the ground is soft, you need to use wooden formwork to do this.

Formwork is a frame (like the sides of a shallow box) made from 1-inch-thick planks. Dig the footing hole and bang in wooden stakes around the edge, so that they are all at the same level. Screw or nail the formwork boards to them, edge uppermost (the stakes are on the outside of the box).

Footings

What is a footing?

A footing is a construction below ground that distributes the weight of a structure so that it is spread over a greater area. It might help to think of the footing as a raft, and the soil as water—a substance that moves and swells. You can then say that the footing keeps a structure afloat, in that it stops it from sinking into the soil. The basic rule of making a footing is the greater the load, the larger the footing needed.

WHY ARE FOOTINGS NEEDED?

Soil is constantly on the move. Depending upon where you live, it swells, slides, and heaves when it is wet or frozen, and shrinks, sinks, and ripples when it is dry. A footing acts to spread the load of the structure it supports in such a way that the wall or patio is unaffected by the movement.

The softer the soil and the heavier the structure being built, the larger the footing needs to be. For small walls in the garden that are no more than 28 inches high, a single-brick-thick wall needs a concrete slab that is 4 inches thick and twice the width of the wall; while a two-brick-thick wall requires a concrete slab that is 6 inches thick and three times the width of the wall.

WHEN ARE THEY NOT NEEDED?

If your site is virgin rock or chalk (meaning that it has never been disturbed), then for small garden structures, such as walls and patios, you can get away without a concrete footing slab. However, if your site is solid rock and slightly sloping, you will either have to level it out with a wedge-shaped raft of concrete, or build raised decking that floats over the slope (by setting posts in holes full of concrete).

With a footing

Concrete — Paving slabs
Hardpan

↗ *The weight of the patio and the load it carries are distributed over a wide area. (Walls need deeper, wider footings.)*

Without a footing

Soil sinks — Slab slides — Sand shifts

↗ *The subsoil shifts under the weight of the patio, causing it to crack, sink, and gradually spread.*

SOIL TYPES AND DRAINAGE

Soil in the average garden usually conforms to these types: sand, clay, heavy loam, or a mixture. All soil types have their problems—sand drains well but shifts, clay holds water and is always on the move, and so on. For the most part, you do need to build a footing, and you have to consider drainage. Dig the footing area to the required depth. If the earth in the bottom is soft, remove it and replace with a layer of compacted hardpan. Lay the concrete slab.

WHAT IF I AM NOT SURE?

If, after digging a few test holes, you are not sure what is going on—maybe the subsoil looks a bit wet and clay-like, and there is a little water in the hole—it is best to go for a generous footing slab. Dig the footing hole to a depth of 20 inches, put down 8 inches of compacted hardpan, and top it off with 12 inches of concrete. Ask the advice of a local builder if you are concerned.

QUICK FOOTINGS THAT WORK WELL

If test holes reveal that the subsoil is firm, stony and well drained, some structures (such as brick patios and paths) can be built on a footing of ballast over hardpan. Dig the footing to a depth of 10 inches, put down 4 inches of compacted hardpan, followed by 4 inches of compacted ballast, and top with the bricks set on 2 inches of raked soft sand. The hardpan and ballast should be compacted with a power tamper to make firm and stable layers.

SUB-BASE MATERIALS

Your choice of sub-base materials will, to a great extent, relate to the tried and trusted traditions in your area.

Hoggin ~ Crushed stone and clay. A good material for well-drained ground—it packs down to a dense layer.

Hardpan ~ Builders' rubble. It should preferably be made up from crushed bricks and tiles (no concrete, plaster, glass, wood, or vegetable matter). Good for soil that needs drainage.

Scalpings ~ Crushed stone in various sizes—a very cheap material in some areas. Good for drainage.

Ballast ~ Coarse sand, small stones, and crushed rock (down to dust size). Compacts to a dense, hard surface—good over hardpan for a brick or paver patio built on firm ground.

USEFUL FOOTINGS

Basic patio and path footing
for bricks, pavers, and small slabs on firm ground

↘ *If the footing hole you have dug is crisp-sided with a dry base, the ground is firm and well drained. If it is a virgin site, compacted ballast over compacted hardpan is generally sufficient, and concrete is not required.*

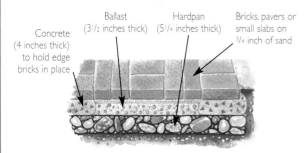

Concrete (4 inches thick) to hold edge bricks in place
Ballast (3 1/2 inches thick)
Hardpan (5 1/4 inches thick)
Bricks, pavers or small slabs on 3/4 inch of sand

Retained patio or path footing
for bricks, pavers, and small slabs on built-up ground

↘ *If the ground has been built up (perhaps a slope has been made from extra earth or ballast), the retaining walls need to be two bricks thick, and the footings for the walls should descend below the level of the built-up ground.*

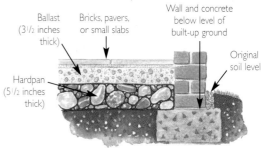

Ballast (3 1/2 inches thick)
Bricks, pavers, or small slabs
Wall and concrete below level of built-up ground
Original soil level
Hardpan (5 1/2 inches thick)

Extra-solid footing
for any patio or path on suspect ground

↘ *If the ground appears to be soft and spongy, the only safe way to proceed is to assume the worst and go for an extra-deep footing with good drainage, using hardpan and water pipes. On top of this, lay a concrete slab with steel mesh sandwiched in it.*

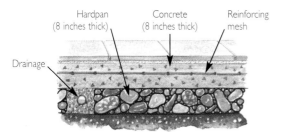

Hardpan (8 inches thick)
Concrete (8 inches thick)
Reinforcing mesh
Drainage

Simple footing for a few steps
on firm ground

↘ *If the ground is firm and stable, and you want to build a flight of three or four brick and slab steps, a simple footing of concrete over hardpan is adequate.*

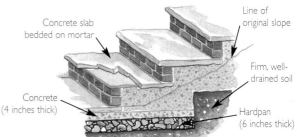

Concrete slab bedded on mortar
Line of original slope
Firm, well-drained soil
Concrete (4 inches thick)
Hardpan (6 inches thick)

WHAT KIND OF PATIO FOOTING DO I NEED?

Patio type	Type of footing required
Bricks on firm ground	Dig a 12-inch-deep footing, lay 6 inches of compacted hardpan, top with 4 inches of compacted ballast followed by a thin layer of sand. Lay the bricks, pour silver sand into the joints, and use a power tamper to vibrate the patio to a firm, stable finish.
Pavers on an old concrete base	Working on the outer edge of the slab, set a level ring of pavers on a stiff mix of concrete. Cover the ring with sharp sand up to the bottom of the pavers. Set the surface pavers in place, trickle silver sand into the joints, and use a power tamper.
Natural bark on wet ground	Dig out the footing to a depth of 8 inches and spread a layer of hardpan or shingle, 4 inches thick. Cover the shingle with a sheet of woven weed-stop plastic. Cover the plastic with 4 inches of crushed bark and roll to a smooth finish.
Concrete slabs on wet ground	Dig a footing 16 inches deep and lay a pattern of perforated plastic water pipes (4 inches in diameter), all pointing to the lowest part of the site. Cover with 8 inches of shingle topped with 4 inches of ballast (both compacted). Lay the slabs on blobs of mortar.
Raised decking on firm ground	Mark out the site in a 20-inch grid and dig 16-inch-deep holes at all the intersections. Put hardpan in each hole and ram it to a firm finish, 4 inches thick. Set pressure-treated posts in the holes and prop them level. Top up the holes with concrete.
Fine gravel on firm, uneven ground	Edge the site with formwork: pressure-treated board, 8 inches wide and 1 inch thick, fixed to level wooden pegs. Spread hardpan over the site and pound it to a compacted finish, 4 inches thick. Fill the formwork with well-washed fine gravel.

Problems with the site

What do I do if I have problems?

If you have considered, planned, and designed the project as described in previous pages, any problems that crop up should only be small ones—just tiny details that you have overlooked. These last-minute hitches are easily rectified, simply by standing back and taking a fresh look at the situation, and then making small alterations. Some sites and situations are potentially more problematic, however; ways to head off trouble are described below.

SMALL SPACES

If you would like to create a patio in a small space, for example a narrow garden about 10 feet wide with high walls all around, it is best not to try and squeeze a small patio into a small garden, but instead to turn the whole garden into one large patio.

LOOKING UPWARD

If you cannot spread outward, how about upward? Hang or grow plants on walls, disguising the boundaries of the area and giving the impression that there is more space.

DARK SPACES

With the right concealed lighting, a small, dark, unexciting space can become a place of mystery and promise. Turn it into a shrine, secret place, cavern, or retreat.

By building upward, this seaside home cleverly fits two complementary patios into the garden without losing any extra space. The raised patio is a haven for sunbathing and enjoying the view, and the lower patio provides a shady escape from the sun.

A WINDY, EXPOSED SITE

A site may have a wonderful view, but be at the mercy of the wind. You have four options: build elsewhere, plant a fast-growing hedge, build a sunken patio with a bank around it, so that the wind whips over your head, or, best of all (if you have the money) build a feature wall on the exposed side.

SLOPING SITES

If a site has a gentle slope, you can build a retaining wall and level the site with hardpan or ballast. If the slope is extreme, the most exciting option is to build a raised decking patio that straddles the slope like a seaside pier.

ALMOST RIGHT, BUT NOT QUITE

The "almost-right-but-not-quite" scenario can only be solved with the passing of time. If you know something is not right, but cannot quite put your finger on the problem, it is best to live with the patio for a while and hope that over time, you will gradually be able to assess faults and put them right.

SURPLUS OF READY-MIXED CONCRETE

If you have ordered too much ready-mixed concrete, there are three sensible options. You can swiftly dig out a footing for a new construction—a path or shed—and cast a concrete slab, or you can donate it to a neighbor. The most unappealing option is to cast it into small, portable blobs and take these to the tip.

An artist's retreat complete with a dramatic raised decking patio built to take advantage of a spectacular view over an estuary. Raised decking easily copes with problems caused by a steeply sloping site such as this.

CONSULT THE PATIO SITE DOCTOR

Digging a hole is not always as straightforward as you might imagine. The exciting thing about pushing a spade into the ground is the unpredictability of what it will reveal. Of all the problems involved with building patios, those associated with digging the footings are the most common. One moment you are digging a hole, and the next moment something happens and a problem rears its ugly head. Don't go into a dizzy panic, but stand back and look at the problem, list possible solutions, and then act accordingly. If the worst comes to the worst and the problem seems totally insurmountable, get professional advice.

If possible, try to avoid problems by looking at site plans and making checks for drains, water pumps, wells, gas pipes, and power cables before you finally settle on a location.

Problem	Solution
You are digging a hole, you chop through something hard, the hole fills with black, foul-smelling water.	If the water is black, the likelihood is that you have chopped through a land drain or soakaway pipe. Wait until the water stops rising, and then use a bucket to bale out the hole. If you see a damaged pottery drain, bridge the hole with a sheet of tin and cover it with concrete.
You are digging a hole and you discover a massive tree root just below the surface of the ground.	Being very careful not to damage the root, ring it (giving it a wide berth) with a mini brick wall and fill the central area with earth topped with shingle. The wall and shingle will become an attractive feature, rather like a piece of sculpture.
You are digging a hole and discover concrete footings just below the surface of the ground.	You can save time and money by incorporating the old footings into the new. If the footings are totally unexpected and look very old, perhaps even ancient, make contact with a local history society before you proceed.
You are digging a hole and chop through a main water pipe—there is fresh water gushing out.	You need to turn off the water supply. Go out into the road, just by the front gate but still on your property, and look for a small iron lid that conceals the mains tap. Lift the lid and turn off the tap. Call the emergency number for the water company immediately.
You are digging a hole and come across a trench lined and bridged with slabs of stone.	The chances are that you have struck an old soakaway trench from a garden septic tank or cesspool, or, if your house is old, from your kitchen sink waste pipe, or even from a local spring. Don't disturb it, simply build over or around it.
You are digging a hole and discover a pit full of builders' rubble.	If the rubble is compacted and full of earth, build the footing over it. If there is a sheet of rusted corrugated iron over the pit, the pit is a rainwater soakaway. Replace the corrugated iron with new, cover it with a slab of concrete and continue work.
You are digging a hole and find a brick well, covered with a stone slab, with water in the bottom.	Wonderful—what a find! Remove the stone slab and lay new bricks on the old to bring the sides of the well above what will be the surface of the patio. When the patio is finished, trim the well with a lid and winding handle and make a feature of it.
You are digging a hole and discover ancient pottery, old coins, and a human skull.	Really exciting—what and who have you found? Stop work immediately and report your find first to the police and then to the local archeological society. Don't carry on digging, don't try to polish up the coins, and don't touch the skull—wait until they have been assessed by professionals.
You are digging a hole and come across a huge boulder as big as a giant pumpkin.	Remove the earth until all the sides of the rock are revealed, and then little by little, with an iron bar and wedges, lever it out of the hole. When the patio is finished, bring the rock back on site and make it into a feature, as might be used in a Japanese garden.
You are digging a hole and fine sand pours out of the sides of the hole.	The sand indicates that the subsoil is unstable and not suitable for digging holes. It is best to build a raft of concrete on the ground. Spread a layer of concrete, 4 inches thick, set a sheet of iron mesh on top of it, then lay another 4 inches of concrete.

Patio shapes and styles

Are there lots of patio styles to choose from?

Patios have come a long way since the grim old days when the best you could hope for was eight concrete paving slabs and a couple of beach chairs. Today you can have a patio in just about any shape, style, and size that you like. A patio is now required to be more than just a dry, level area—it is a garden room where you can relax, have a barbecue, spend time with family and friends, and enjoy a view of the garden for many months of the year.

PATIO SHAPES

Plan the shape of the patio to suit your needs. What is the patio going to be used for? Do you want it to relate to the shape of the garden? Do you want it to reflect the character of the house? Do you have strong preferences for certain materials? How much money do you want to spend? Your answers to these questions will, to a great extent, decide the shape and character of the patio that you build.

Basic rectangular

↗ *A modest rectangular patio set close to (and square with) the house. It is level with the lawn and a good option for a small garden.*

Rectangular combinations

↗ *An L-shaped patio, made from two linked rectangles, level with the lawn. It is designed to fit around existing features.*

Circular (also hexagonal, octagonal)

↗ *Strong shapes—such as circles and hexagons—are attractive and decorative. They make beautiful island patios in a large sea of lawn, trees, shrubs, and flower borders.*

Geometrical combinations

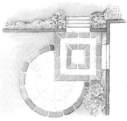

↗ *Geometrical combinations, for example circles joined to rectangles, or linked circles, are not only wonderfully dynamic in their own right, but can be used to create small patio "rooms."*

Organic

↗ *An informal, flowing shape can look perfect in a large wild garden, making a natural sitting area that is like a clearing.*

Complex

↗ *Complex forms are good when you need to create a number of small areas at different levels to suit a steeply sloping site.*

Split levels and shape

Linked shapes let you create split-level areas. So, for example, you might have a circle linked to a rectangle, with the rectangle forming the main "room" of the patio, and the circle making a smaller "room" slightly raised to one side. This linked split-level two-room design, with one room approached by a small flight of steps, creates a private area, like an intimate den. (See page 38.)

PATIO STYLES

Just like castles, houses, and cottages, patios can be designed to relate to a regional or historical style. If you enjoy all things French, Mediterranean, or Swiss, delight in English seaside style, or have a passion for Victoriana or the American Wild West, there's no reason at all why your patio cannot use that style as a reference point.

↗ *A porch decking patio with a Mediterranean feel. Angular raised beds made of bleached wood host a minimalistic planting scheme. Azure gravel surrounds the plants, providing a practical mulch, but also echoing the shimmering colors of sea and sky.*
↖ *A traditional patio in the Old English cottage style, given a modern twist by the addition of contemporary furniture. The patio is slightly raised to cope with a sloping site.*

PATIO STYLES AND THEMES

STYLE / THEME	TYPICAL MATERIALS / COMPONENTS
Old English Cottage A style that was popular in England and America in the 1930s.	*Lots of red brick and tile surfaces, columns, arbors, stone ball finials, and formal fishponds. A high standard of bricklaying expertise, with central steps running down to a lawn. Vegetable garden and lots of roses.*
American Wild West Images familiar from American cowboy movies.	*Lots of decking: a board patio hard against the house, covered with a porch and surrounded with balustrades made up of fretted boards. Wooden steps, water barrel, gingerbread trim, picket fences, and lots of white paint. Simple flower borders.*
Japanese Garden A calm, ordered look inspired by nature and the tea ceremony.	*An area of flagstones, with a wooden walkway running across a stream. Large feature rocks, collections of stones, cobblestones, and raked sand or gravel. Ferns, moss, stone water bowls and troughs, willow, bamboo, and bonsai trees.*
English Seaside A retro design framework from the seaside culture of the 1950s.	*An area of raised decking with a narrow wooden pier or walkway and a cobblestone and sand beach. Deckchairs, striped canvas awning, fairy lights strung between posts, benches with cast-iron ends. Grasses, driftwood, and glass fishing floats.*
Mediterranean Hotel Whitewashed walls, bright flowers; a snapshot of a sun-drenched retreat.	*A level, paved area with rendered and white-painted block walls to the sides. Raised pools, café chairs and tables, bleached wood benches. Simple, clean lines, modern lighting. Gravel, colored tiles, raised beds with drought-tolerant planting.*
Old Spanish Courtyard Stylish and intricate North African references: mysterious and striking.	*A private courtyard area with high walls to the sides and a low, formal pond at the center. Lots of symmetry and surfaces decorated with ceramic mosaics in geometrical patterns, circles, triangles, and zigzags. A Moorish arch feature.*

Quick patios

Is it possible to build a patio on a weekend?

Much depends upon your skills and motivation, and how many friends you can rope in to help, but if you spend a week or so making plans and preparing the ground, there is no reason at all why you cannot complete a patio on a long weekend. It would be hard work, and mean starting the project last thing on the Friday, and continuing through Saturday and Sunday, but by the Monday you could be lying flat out on the patio!

QUICK GRAVEL PATIO

If your site is more or less level, gravel is an easy option.

Start by removing the turf and digging down about 8 inches. Pile the topsoil around the sides and use a spade and rake to sculpt it into a long, low mound. Edge the excavated area with 8-inch-wide wooden boards, so that they stand clear by about 4 inches.

Fill the recess with 4 inches of compacted hardpan and top it with 4 inches of washed fine gravel. Turf the mound. Furnish the patio with a picnic table, benches, deckchairs, and a barbecue. Arrange pot plants around the sides.

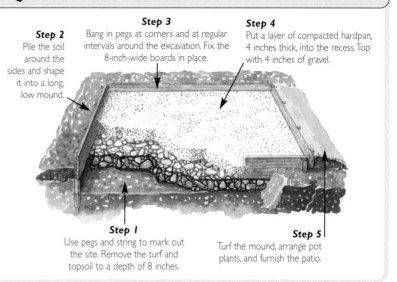

Step 2
Pile the soil around the sides and shape it into a long, low mound.

Step 3
Bang in pegs at corners and at regular intervals around the excavation. Fix the 8-inch-wide boards in place.

Step 4
Put a layer of compacted hardpan, 4 inches thick, into the recess. Top with 4 inches of gravel.

Step 1
Use pegs and string to mark out the site. Remove the turf and topsoil to a depth of 8 inches.

Step 5
Turf the mound, arrange pot plants, and furnish the patio.

QUICK DECKING PATIO

Decide on the size of the patio and divide it up into a 1-yard grid, like a checkerboard. Clear the turf away from the site.

Dig 8-inch-deep holes at the corners and grid intersections. Half-fill the holes with hardpan. Cover the site with woven plastic sheeting. Dig away the earth from around the holes and set concrete blocks on the hardpan, using mortar to ensure that they are all at the same level.

Use treated 2 x 8-inch wood to build a framework. Sit the framework on the concrete blocks. Cover the frame with 4-inch-wide boards nailed 1/4 inch apart.

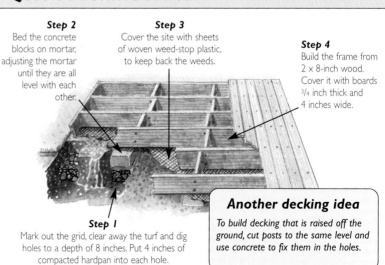

Step 2
Bed the concrete blocks on mortar, adjusting the mortar until they are all level with each other.

Step 3
Cover the site with sheets of woven weed-stop plastic, to keep back the weeds.

Step 4
Build the frame from 2 x 8-inch wood. Cover it with boards 3/4 inch thick and 4 inches wide.

Step 1
Mark out the grid, clear away the turf and dig holes to a depth of 8 inches. Put 4 inches of compacted hardpan into each hole.

Another decking idea

To build decking that is raised off the ground, cut posts to the same level and use concrete to fix them in the holes.

QUICK FOOTINGS FOR PAVED PATIOS

There are two swift ways of laying patio slabs: on a stiff mix of concrete, or on compacted sand. Both require a similar footing and preparation.

Mark out the site and clear the turf and topsoil down to a depth of 8 inches. Bang 12-inch-long wooden pegs into the ground so that they all stand level and are 6 inches clear of the bottom of the excavation.

Spread 4 inches of compacted hardpan over the site. Set the slabs on compacted sand or concrete, according to method 1 or 2.

→ *Prepare the site and spread 4 inches of compacted hardpan. Top with compacted sharp sand to the level of the top of the pegs. Set the slabs level on the sand, laying each slab on five large blobs of mortar.*

Method 1
Slabs on compacted sand

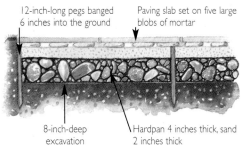

12-inch-long pegs banged 6 inches into the ground

Paving slab set on five large blobs of mortar

8-inch-deep excavation

Hardpan 4 inches thick, sand 2 inches thick

Method 2
Slabs on concrete

→ *Prepare the site and spread 4 inches of compacted hardpan. Spread a dryish, stiff mix of concrete to the level of the top of the pegs. Carefully position the slabs directly on the moist concrete.*

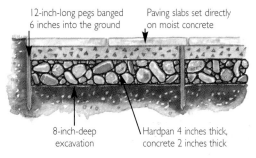

12-inch-long pegs banged 6 inches into the ground

Paving slabs set directly on moist concrete

8-inch-deep excavation

Hardpan 4 inches thick, concrete 2 inches thick

Wet or clay ground

If the ground consists of clay or is wet, dig out the footing to 16 inches, and increase the depth of hardpan to 8 inches. Top this with 4 inches of concrete, inserting a metal rod mesh in the concrete for reinforcement. Set the slabs on blobs of mortar.

GOOD DESIGN CAN SAVE YOU EFFORT

Rectangular shapes are much easier to build than circles or hexagons. Design the patio so that it uses a number of whole units—bricks, concrete slabs, pavers, decking boards, or whatever. If the site is sloping, avoid heavy digging and concrete mixing by going for raised decking. As far as possible, design the patio so that it uses local materials, because this will cut effort and costs.

GOOD PLANNING CAN SAVE YOU TIME

Order all the materials weeks beforehand. Plan the project so that you can complete it in good weather. Clear and prepare the site well ahead of the actual building work. Cover the area immediately around the site with workboards and tarpaulins, so that you don't do irreparable damage to the lawn. Make sure that you have all the tools that you need. Plan the work in day-length chunks.

GETTING EXTRA HELP

Canvass help from family and friends well ahead, so that they can plan their time accordingly. If the task is really daunting, get a contractor to do some of the heavy work, such as digging the footings and compacting the hardpan. If you are asking friends to help, make sure that they have the correct tools for the job. Make sure that all your workers have protective gloves.

USING MACHINES TO SPEED UP THE WORK

Renting a machine might seem to be an extra cost, but it can save money by cutting down your work time. An power concrete mixer is a boon for mixing concrete. A power tamper is great when you have to compact a lot of hardpan. If you are building wooden decking, a power miter saw (chop saw) and one or more battery-driven screwdrivers will save you hours of hard work.

IS YOUR QUICK PATIO SAFE TO USE?

A patio must be safe, with no slippery slabs, badly built steps, or uneven paving slabs waiting to trip you up. If you have any doubts at all about the suitability of materials or the size of fixings required, seek professional advice. Most builders' yards are happy to give guidance.

MORE QUICK PATIOS

Soft sand ~ A large area of soft sand makes a good patio for a family with toddlers—it is easy to build, safe and fun to use. You just dig out a shallow hole and fill it with clean sand.

Crushed bark ~ Crushed bark is wonderful for a natural patio with a forest-glade effect—it is firm and dry underfoot, easy to build, economical, safe for children, and eco-friendly.

Decking boards ~ Decking squares set in fine gravel make a fast, easy patio. Great for a temporary patio.

Basic patios

How do I make a basic rectangular patio?

If you enjoy simple garden structures that are solidly built and will last a lifetime, a basic no-frills rectangular patio is an appropriate choice. There are three good options: a patio made from concrete paving slabs, a decking patio made from regular decking boards (will suit a small, modern garden), and a patio made from kiln-fired clay bricks (excellent for creating a traditional-looking patio suitable for the garden of a cottage or townhouse).

HOW TO BUILD A BASIC PATIO OUT OF CONCRETE PAVERS

Several shapes of reconstituted stone slab, which look convincingly like the real thing, have been used for this patio.

Choose your slab type, measure its size, and decide how big you want the patio to be (in whole slabs).

Use pegs and string to mark the area on the ground. Remove the turf and topsoil to a depth of 8 inches. Take a number of 12-inch-long wooden pegs and hammer them (at 3-foot intervals over the site) into the ground so that they are level and stand proud by 6 inches.

Cover the site with 4 inches of compacted hardpan topped by 1½ inches of compacted sharp sand and ½ inch of soft sand. Finally, ease the slabs into place and fill the joints between them with silver sand.

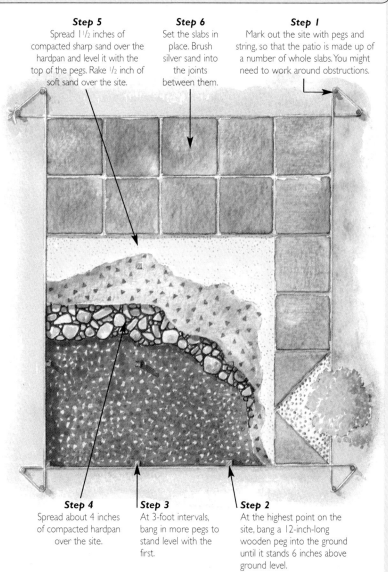

Step 5
Spread 1½ inches of compacted sharp sand over the hardpan and level it with the top of the pegs. Rake ½ inch of soft sand over the site.

Step 6
Set the slabs in place. Brush silver sand into the joints between them.

Step 1
Mark out the site with pegs and string, so that the patio is made up of a number of whole slabs. You might need to work around obstructions.

Step 4
Spread about 4 inches of compacted hardpan over the site.

Step 3
At 3-foot intervals, bang in more pegs to stand level with the first.

Step 2
At the highest point on the site, bang a 12-inch-long wooden peg into the ground until it stands 6 inches above ground level.

HOW TO BUILD A BASIC PATIO OUT OF DECKING

This simple patio made of decking tiles adjoins a seaside cabin. Slight variations in shade between the tiles add interest.

➜ Raised decking is a good option for sloping ground, or where you have to work over things such as drains and old footings. Use 4-inch-square section for the posts, 2 x 8-inch for the beams and joists, and 1 x 4-inch for the boards.

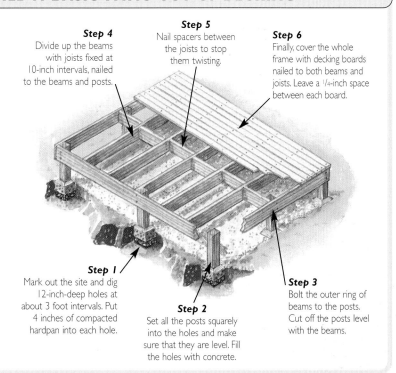

Step 4
Divide up the beams with joists fixed at 10-inch intervals, nailed to the beams and posts.

Step 5
Nail spacers between the joists to stop them twisting.

Step 6
Finally, cover the whole frame with decking boards nailed to both beams and joists. Leave a 1/4-inch space between each board.

Step 1
Mark out the site and dig 12-inch-deep holes at about 3 foot intervals. Put 4 inches of compacted hardpan into each hole.

Step 2
Set all the posts squarely into the holes and make sure that they are level. Fill the holes with concrete.

Step 3
Bolt the outer ring of beams to the posts. Cut off the posts level with the beams.

HOW TO BUILD A BASIC PATIO OUT OF BRICKS

A traditional patio made from high-fired bricks. The herringbone design—with the bricks set square to the sides—keeps brick-cutting to a minimum.

← ↘ A brick patio is expensive; however it is easy to build, attractive, and will last a lifetime. Mark out the site and remove the turf and topsoil. Ring the site with a mini brick wall, then fill the central area with compacted hardpan topped with compacted sharp sand and raked soft sand. Lay the bricks in position and fill the joints with silver sand. Finally, use a power tamper to settle the bricks into place.

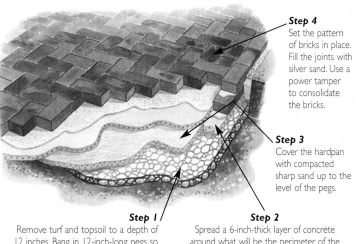

Step 4
Set the pattern of bricks in place. Fill the joints with silver sand. Use a power tamper to consolidate the bricks.

Step 3
Cover the hardpan with compacted sharp sand up to the level of the pegs.

Step 1
Remove turf and topsoil to a depth of 12 inches. Bang in 12-inch-long pegs so that they stand 6 inches proud. Spread 4 inches of compacted hardpan.

Step 2
Spread a 6-inch-thick layer of concrete around what will be the perimeter of the patio, and set the edge bricks in place so that they are level with each other.

Real stone patios

Real quarried stone is more expensive than reconstituted stone (a mixture of crushed stone and concrete), but its beauty as a material is hard to match. To build a patio from it involves a lot of hard work moving heavy slabs of stone. Once a real stone patio is in place, it transcends fads and fashions and will last a lifetime. This type of patio will slot equally well into a traditional or modern garden, with the ability to blend into any decorative scheme.

To save money, this patio has been made from salvaged stone. Instead of obscuring the attractive stone surface with lots of containers, plants tumble from hanging baskets.

Real stone tips

The secret of working with stone is to do your best to use the pieces as you find them, and keep cutting to a minimum. Salvaged stone, which could be described as stone that has been worked by someone else, is good from this point of view. It varies in thickness, so needs to be set on generous blobs of mortar.

FOOTINGS

To provide a firm base for a real stone patio, the footing ideally needs to be dug to a depth of 12 inches, filled with 10 inches of compacted hardpan, and topped with 2 inches of concrete. Each slab is set on mortar (one blob at each corner and in the center); joints are filled with mortar.

ADVANTAGES AND DISADVANTAGES

Advantages of real stone

✔ Looks good in its own right and doesn't need to be treated or painted.

✔ Lasts a lifetime.

✔ The color doesn't fade and just looks better with the passing years.

✔ It makes very attractive cleft-stone paving—a design solution perfect for those who enjoy attention to detail.

Disadvantages of real stone

✘ Real stone slabs are expensive.

✘ Delivery and handling costs are high.

✘ It must be laid on a solid footing of compacted hardpan and concrete, and pointed with mortar.

✘ Real stone slabs are very heavy—you need to be strong and fit, and you might need help with the lifting.

OPTIONS FOR REAL STONE PATIOS

Real stone pavers

Though pavers made from real cut stone are both expensive and difficult to source, they are an exciting option.

Reclaimed stone with gravel gaps

Reclaimed flagstones, set together for best fit, with the joints between them filled with fine gravel and planted with herbs.

Cleft-stone paving

Cleft-stone paving is a good choice if you want a relatively cheap patio. The stone is bedded on blobs of mortar.

Stone blocks

Stone blocks come in many types and sizes. Salvaged stone blocks from city roads may be available from local councils.

Decorative combinations

Brick and stone look really good together— perfect if you want to create a low-cost patio for your garden.

Random, worn-top field stones, set together for best fit, with the wide courses planted with grass and wild flowers.

TYPES OF REAL STONE

Slate
Gray to brown, smooth and shiny. Breaks easily into flat pieces.

Sandstone
Gold through to green, with a sandy texture. Breaks into flat pieces.

Limestone
White and soft. Reclaimed stone is good for walls and edge detailing.

Granite
Gray to green, with some sparkly bits. Reclaimed stone is very attractive.

When you go to look at real stone at a builders' supplier or reclamation yard, you will be presented with lots of types, such as "York stone" or "Pennsylvania stone." Don't worry about the names, other than to find out whether the stone is slate, sandstone, limestone, or granite. If the stone is hard, a pleasant color, and has at least one flat face, it is suitable for use in a patio. Slate is good because it splits naturally into thin, flat pieces and is a good color. Sandstone splits well, is an appealing color, and has a very attractive sandy texture. Limestone works well as small pieces for walls and steps, but looks a bit slick as large slabs. Granite stone blocks are perfect for patios and paths.

HOW TO BUILD A CLEFT-STONE PAVING PATIO

Try to arrange the stones so that the gaps are a similar width

Fill (point) the gaps with mortar

Build a footing using 8 inches of compacted hardpan topped with 2 inches of sharp sand. Practice arranging a small area to see how the pieces of stone will fit together best. Although you can cut or break stone to fit (see page 71), keep cutting to a minimum. Use big pieces in the middle and smaller pieces toward the outside. Set the stones on a generous layer of a dryish mix of concrete. Point the gaps with mortar. (See page 39 for how to build a circular cleft-stone paving patio.)

HOW TO LAY REAL STONE SLABS

↘ Dig out the earth where the patio will be situated to a depth of 6 inches. Level the site. Set each slab on a dryish mix of concrete (concrete that has been mixed with the minimum of water). Level the slabs with each other. Use a trowel to fill the joints with mortar. For another construction method with an even more solid footing, see the "Footings" box on page 26.

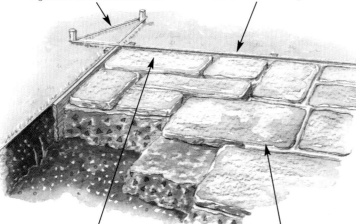

Step 1
Use a tape measure, pegs, and string to set out the area on the ground. Dig out the earth and level the area.

Step 2
Put down boards to make formwork (defines the patio's shape and contains the footing).

Step 3
Concentrating on one slab at a time, put down a shovelful of concrete about 5 inches thick, set the slab in place, and adjust the level.

Step 4
When the concrete under the slabs is dry, use a small mason's trowel to fill the joints with a dryish mix of mortar.

HOW TO BUILD A PATIO USING STONE BLOCKS

Reclaimed granite stone block

Dry-mix mortar brushed into joints

Generous amount of mortar

8 inches of compacted hardpan topped with a skim of sand

Fill the footing with hardpan and cover with sand. One block at a time, spread a layer of mortar over the sand and press the block into the mortar. Aim for the mortar to be about 1½ inches lower than the top of the blocks. Brush dry-mix mortar into the joints.

USEFUL TIPS

- Be generous with the hardpan and make sure it is well compacted.
- Old bricks make perfect hardpan.
- Use sharp sand, not soft (or builder's) and make sure it is well compacted.
- For large areas, it's worth renting a power tamper to vibrate the hardpan and sand into place.
- If you can't afford real stone, consider using reconstituted stone. Some of the modern products are good enough to fool the eye into believing that they are the genuine article.

Reconstituted stone patios

Is reconstituted stone as good as real stone?

Reconstituted stone consists of concrete plus an aggregate of ground-up stone. At one time, reconstituted stone was rather unattractive, with a uniform texture and available only in a selection of harsh colors. However, modern reconstituted stone is so convincing that it is almost impossible to tell it apart from the genuine article. Stone pavers are particularly good—colors, cast patterns, and textures vary from slab to slab to give a realistic effect.

ADVANTAGES AND DISADVANTAGES

Advantages of reconstituted stone

- ✔ Readily available in lots of grades, textures, colors, and sizes.
- ✔ It is many times less expensive than real stone—a fraction of the cost.
- ✔ Because it is a uniform size and thickness, it is perfect for a patio.
- ✔ It doesn't have a grain, so cannot be damaged by extremes in temperature.

Disadvantages of reconstituted stone

- ✘ The colors of some low-grade types can fade over time—sometimes in just a couple of years.
- ✘ It doesn't have the subtle texture of real stone—there are no sparkly bits on sides and edges.
- ✘ It doesn't age as well as real stone, and doesn't develop a delicate patina and textural subtlety.

FOOTINGS

Just like real stone, reconstituted stone needs a good, solid footing. (See page 16 for more about footings.)

A medium-sized patio made from reconstituted stone slabs. Note the subtle textures and the way the random design is made up from a number of modules consisting of different slabs—a large square, a quarter-square, and a rectangle.

HOW TO LAY RECONSTITUTED STONE SLABS ON FIRM GROUND

↘ Dig the patio footing: remove the earth to a depth of 6 inches. Level the site. Set each slab on a dryish mix of concrete (concrete that has been mixed with the minimum of water). Level the slabs with each other. Use a trowel to fill the joints with mortar. For another construction method with an even more solid footing, see the "Footings" box on page 26.

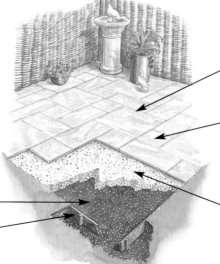

Step 5
When the concrete has set, use a small trowel to tool mortar into the joints. Finally, when the mortar has partly set, use a brush to clean the joints.

Step 4
Standing on a plank or workboard, carefully set the pavers in place. Level and adjust each slab as you go.

Step 3
Working from one side to another, spread a dryish mix of concrete, 4 inches thick, over the whole site. Level and tamp the concrete with a long board.

Step 1
Use a tape measure, pegs and string to set out the area on the ground. Dig out the earth to a depth of 6 inches..

Step 2
Edge the excavation with 6-inch-wide boards, pegged and nailed into place.

OPTIONS FOR RECONSTITUTED STONE PATIOS

Colors and textures

   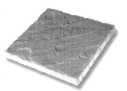

Weathered stone is a silver-gray color and looks almost black when it is wet.

Old-style stone—light gray with a touch of green—turns a rich slate gray when it is wet.

Weathered red stone (reddish stone with pools of brick red) looks almost red when wet.

Weathered buff—a hot creamy yellow—ages to a gentle, paler cream.

Other paving components

Slabs that mimic old, weathered bricks are very good for edgings and small details to break up large areas of plain paving.

Designed to look like stone blocks.

Walling blocks can be used to edge a patio (especially effective around raised decking and to edge small, formal ponds).

Slabs designed to look like old terra-cotta tiles are ideal for small details, edges, and steps, when you want to inject some color.

Decorative pavers

This design, with an octagon at the center, makes a wonderful detail set within a large, formal patio made up of square and rectangular slabs.

A pattern of pavers—carefully cut to shape—used to circle a small, round patio and form an overall square shape. Gravel and plants frame the shape and give added visual emphasis.

CUTTING PAVERS

First, cut a groove across the slab.

It is best to cut reconstituted stone pavers with a power angle grinder. You will also need a brick chisel and a stonemason's hammer. Start by marking the line of cut with chalk. Wearing protective goggles, a dust mask, and gloves, use the grinder to cut a groove, ⅛ inch deep, across the slab. Cut the groove slightly deeper at the corners.

Sit the slab on the grass. Now, with a brick chisel in one hand and a stonemason's hammer in the other, set the chisel on the groove and give it a series of light taps with the hammer. If you are doing it correctly, you will hear the sound gradually change, until the slab suddenly breaks into two pieces. Don't rush the process, and don't be tempted to give the slab a single blow.

Use a brick chisel to break the slab.

Useful tips

Take your time choosing materials and putting down a footing, and you won't be disappointed with the patio that results.

Color fast ~ Make sure when you are buying reconstituted slabs that the colors are fast, with the colors running through the thickness of the slab.

Pattern repeats ~ If you look at textured reconstituted stone pavers— the ones that are press-cast to look like specific stone types—you will see that there are perhaps only one or two different designs. Ensure when you set identical slabs side by side that you turn them so that the designs appear different.

Window dressing ~ Consider buying top-quality plain slabs, and make them special by trimming with a feature such as a special brick edging or a mini wall.

Efflorescence (white stain) ~ Thin white stains (a sort of powdery coating) are normal. They will gradually vanish of their own accord. If you wish, efflorescence can be removed with a special wash and the patio then protected with masonry sealant.

Natural patios

Are natural patios difficult to create?

Anatural patio appears to be an easy option, because it is no more than a little haven built using natural materials to imitate nature, decorated with lots of planting. However, this appearance of simplicity is not easy to achieve. The best way to proceed is to find a perfect glade or dell, then do your best to copy its shape and form, and the way it is positioned in relation to the sun. Leave it to time and nature to do the rest, gradually blending it into the landscape.

WHAT ARE NATURAL PATIOS?

A natural patio is a resting place—a sheltered, warm, sunny spot, perhaps with just the right amount of dappled shade; a cozy, dry place that invites you to stop, look and linger. It could reproduce the sort of area that walkers might seek out to take a break, or represent your favorite type of scenery or beauty spot.

For some, the perfect place might be a shingle-covered area by a beach, with rocks and patches of low planting; for others, the ideal retreat would be a forest glade, with a leaf-mold floor, a fallen tree, trees and bushes dotted about, and a sea of bluebells. An old-fashioned meadow, crammed with cornflowers, poppies, and tall grasses waving in a gentle breeze, with a mown area to hide in, might also appeal.

➜ *An area of lawn set within a copse, and designed to look like a natural forest glade, makes a perfect retreat. This patio is cheap to make, so you can afford to spend more on a good quality garden seat.*

NATURAL PATIO OPTIONS

Orchard clearing

↗ This perfect natural patio takes advantage of a beautiful orchard with fruit trees and lush meadow grass. The area forming the patio has been leveled with a thick layer of shingle for drainage, and topped with a layer of wood chips or bark. The huge table (made from a slab of wood) is a permanent feature, and is great for informal meals. The fallen tree is a favorite play area for children.

Pond-side retreat

➜ Patios and ponds make the perfect partners—great if you enjoy watching all the wildlife associated with a pond. The area is defined by large rocks and covered by hardpan topped with fine gravel. The hardpan ensures that there is a dry, level area, which lets you spread a blanket, have a sumptuous picnic, and then stretch out and relax.

Forest hideaway

➜ Robinson Crusoe might have enjoyed this natural patio in a forest clearing, surrounded by trees. The hut blends into the leaf-covered forest floor to make a wonderful hideaway.

HOW TO CREATE A PATIO IN A MATURE ORCHARD

Wait for a warm summer's day, then take a chair into the orchard and sit in what you consider is a good spot. Observe how the sun moves in relation to the trees and existing buildings, and generally look at the area with a view to sitting there with family and friends for an informal meal.

Peg out the area that you want to be level and drained, bearing in mind that people tend to take up more space when they are outdoors. Remove the turf and topsoil and spread a generous layer of compacted and rolled ballast, followed by a sheet of woven weed-stop plastic. Top with crushed bark. For a truly natural look, use tree stumps for tables and seating.

Existing fruit trees
Trees cut back, trimmed and pruned, so that they set the scene. Old trees could be sculpted to provide additional seating.

Wooden bench
Old wooden benches always come in useful and look good, blending into the scene with ease.

Crushed bark
Crushed bark provides the perfect natural surface—it is firm and dry underfoot, safe for children to play on, and biodegradable.

Drained and leveled
Turf and topsoil removed. Layer of compacted and rolled ballast laid and leveled, and covered with plastic sheet. Topped with a thick layer of crushed bark.

Tree stumps
Well-placed tree trunks provide seating for children, while sawn sections provide informal tables and seats for adults.

HOW TO MAKE A SEASIDE-THEMED PATIO

Choose a spot that is dry and exposed, and gets as much sunshine as possible. Remove the turf and topsoil, and level the area with rolled ballast. Cover the ballast with fine crushed rock or shingle.

Buy as many rocks as you can afford (preferably flat with weathered edges and a water-washed appearance). Lay the rocks with generous gaps around them, and fill these with pebbles and sand. Plant a selection of seaside flowers such as sea lavender and thrift. Dress the area with seaside finds such as driftwood, lengths of rope, shells, or even an old rowboat.

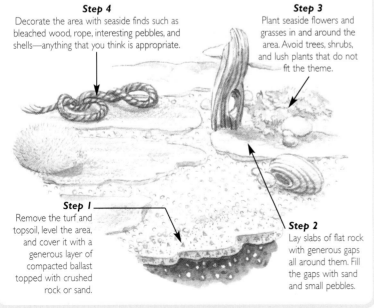

Step 4
Decorate the area with seaside finds such as bleached wood, rope, interesting pebbles, and shells—anything that you think is appropriate.

Step 3
Plant seaside flowers and grasses in and around the area. Avoid trees, shrubs, and lush plants that do not fit the theme.

Step 1
Remove the turf and topsoil, level the area, and cover it with a generous layer of compacted ballast topped with crushed rock or sand.

Step 2
Lay slabs of flat rock with generous gaps all around them. Fill the gaps with sand and small pebbles.

HOW TO CREATE A MEADOW CLEARING

Choose a level spot in an existing lawn and mow a sitting area. Let the surrounding grass grow tall. Plant selected areas with as many species of meadow flowers as you can find. Keep the area clear of nettles and brambles.

Themes and props

A themed natural patio needs to be dressed with the appropriate props, rather like a movie set. Bales of hay and old farm machinery will enhance a meadow; tree stumps and sawhorses will make a forest glade look authentic; rocks, shale, and alpine plants will suit a mountain dell.

Brick or paver patios

Does it take a long time to lay a brick patio?

If you enjoy geometrical patterns, a brick patio is a good project to choose. Because bricks are fairly small, they do take longer to lay than paving slabs, for example. However, working with bricks is a wonderfully therapeutic activity, and there is something really satisfying about the way they fit together. Bricks have six sides: two end or "header" faces, two side or "stretcher" faces, a top or "frog" face, and a bottom face. The pattern bricks are laid in is termed the bond.

TYPES OF CLAY BRICK

Bricks come in hundreds of colors and textures, with an actual size of $8^1/_2$ inches long, 4 inches wide, and $2^1/_2$ inches thick. When calculating quantities for a project, $^1/_2$-inch-thick mortar joints are allowed for, giving a unit measurement of 9 inches long, $4^1/_2$ inches wide and 3 inches thick. For patios, use well-fired (or high-fired) exterior-grade bricks, or engineering bricks, both of which are harder than standard bricks, with low rates of water absorption and good frost resistance.

CONSIDERATIONS

To pave a surface more cheaply, you can use concrete "brick" pavers instead of clay bricks. They will not look as good as clay bricks, but they do the job. If you use clay bricks, you have a choice of laying them either frog face down (so that the plan view size, with mortar joints, is 9 x $4^1/_2$ inches), or stretcher face up (9 x 3 inches). Bear this in mind when you work out the brick pattern and coverage.

Calculating brick quantities

If you lay the bricks stretcher face up (9 x 3 inches), there are five bricks to every 12 inches square. If you lay them frog face down (9 x $4^1/_2$ inches face uppermost), there are three bricks to every 12 inches square.

A standard clay brick plus joints is 9 inches long, $4^1/_2$ inches wide and 3 inches thick

BRICK COMBINATIONS

Bricks are adaptable—they look equally good when they are combined with other materials such as clay tiles, concrete slabs, natural stone, cobblestones, and wood.

A formal pattern of bricks with an infill of cobblestones, gravel, and planting

Old bricks with stone slabs and tiles

A curved sweep of bricks combined with an infill of fine gravel and sand

BRICK PATTERNS

There are many traditional patterns for brick paving (originally called "floor" patterns), some dating back over 400 years. These classic patterns look just as good today.

Running wall bond

Square herringbone bond

Basketweave bond

Running and stack bond

Double basketweave bond

Diagonal herringbone bond

BRICKWORK ADDITIONS

The wonderful thing about building a brickwork patio is the ease of making additions to the project at a later date. If the patio has a good concrete footing, you can furnish it with other brick structures such as boundary walls, pillars, raised borders, seats, a barbecue, or even a raised pond.

A brick raised bed, built directly on the edge of the patio, creates a unified theme. It provides some shelter as well as a planting area.

HOW TO LAY A BRICK PATIO ON SOFT GROUND

If your site is wet and generally spongy and uneven, it is best to lay the bricks on a slab of concrete. This is hard work and adds to the cost of the project, but the concrete will ensure a long-lasting patio, and lets you build additions without worrying about a footing.

Buy ready-mixed concrete (or at least rent a cement mixer—refer to page 12), and recruit some friends to help you with the work.

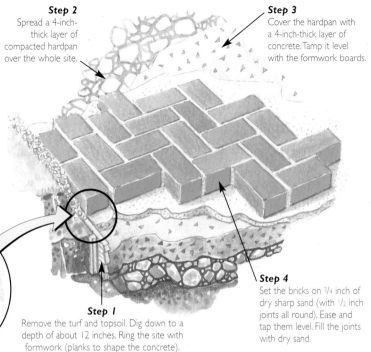

Step 2
Spread a 4-inch-thick layer of compacted hardpan over the whole site.

Step 3
Cover the hardpan with a 4-inch-thick layer of concrete. Tamp it level with the formwork boards.

Step 4
Set the bricks on $3/4$ inch of dry sharp sand (with $1/2$ inch joints all round). Ease and tap them level. Fill the joints with dry sand.

Step 1
Remove the turf and topsoil. Dig down to a depth of about 12 inches. Ring the site with formwork (planks to shape the concrete).

Edge detail (cross-section)

Edge bricks bedded on mortar; remainder on sharp sand

Concrete, 4 inches thick

Compacted hardpan, 4 inches thick

HOW TO LAY A CONCRETE PAVER PATIO ON FIRM, DRY GROUND

If the ground is firm and dry, you may choose to use concrete block pavers to cut costs. These can be laid directly on a bed of sand. An edging is necessary to prevent the pavers from spreading outward.

Remove the turf and dig down to a depth of 8 inches. Shovel a line of stiff concrete around the site and set the edging pavers in position. Use a plank and carpenter's level to ensure that the edging is level—both along the run of the edges and across the site.

Spread a mixture of fine topsoil and hardpan and use a power tamper to compact it to a level finish. Spread 2 inches of sharp sand over the hardpan and compact it to a smooth, level finish. Spread a thin layer of loose sand over the site and arrange the pavers so that they are about $1/2$ inch higher than the edging. Compact the pavers. Finally, spread fine sand over the paving and run the power tamper over the whole site.

Cross-section

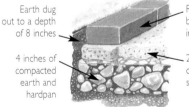

Earth dug out to a depth of 8 inches

Retaining edge blocks set level in concrete

4 inches of compacted earth and hardpan

2 inches of compacted sharp sand

Edges

Bricks set upright to make a strong soldier edge

Bricks set flat down to make a header course edge

Bricks set at an angle to make dog-tooth or Sussex edging

Bullnose bricks set upright to make a decorative edge

Types of block and block patterns

Running wall bond— with joints staggered

Simple stacked side-by-side bond

Double basketweave bond

Herringbone bond set square

Herringbone bond set diagonally

Running hexagon 1-to-2 bond

Decking patios

Can I make a large decking patio on several levels?

Decking is very versatile—it can be used to make a straightforward ground-level patio, or it can easily be built on several levels, like a seaside pier above water, or a forest observation platform. The advantage of decking is the speed of the whole building operation. An area of rugged ground can be swiftly transformed by a decking patio. If you want to build a dramatic patio without too much site disturbance, and you are in a hurry, decking is the answer.

The perfect decking patio, perched high above the ground in order to accommodate the site, take advantage of a beautiful woodland view, and facilitate birdwatching.

ADVANTAGES AND DISADVANTAGES

Advantages of a decking patio

✔ The site does not need leveling—posts of different lengths cope with the slope of the ground.

✔ The materials are easier to handle than those for a concrete slab patio.

✔ It can be built over utilities (water, gas, and electricity supply pipes).

✔ Generally, the materials aren't as invasive as brick and concrete.

Disadvantages of a decking patio

✘ With care, wooden decking can last for 25 years, but a brick patio will last for several lifetimes.

✘ Decking patios require a lot of maintenance—washing, treating, and general running repairs.

Grooved decking

Grooved decking is readily available in Europe, where it is favored because it is considered to be an anti-slip surface. In the USA, however, it is something of a rarity and only available by special order.

DECKING DESIGN OPTIONS

Attached to house

↗ *This patio has been raised above the ground so that it relates to the house.*

Separate from house

↗ *A deck built close to the water's edge, so that it can be used as an observation pier.*

Split-level

↗ *Decks raised one above another to step over an old footing.*

Customized shape

↗ *Decking can be built to almost any shape.*

Patterned

↗ *The wood can be fixed in a variety of patterns.*

Cut-out area

↗ *Decking built to take advantage of a special tree.*

Individual

↗ *Decking designed as an eye-catching feature, to mirror an existing circular stone patio and a large, round millstone.*

BASIC DECKING CONSTRUCTION SEQUENCE

1 Prepare the ground

Measure out the plan view on the ground, marking the post holes no more than 5 feet apart. Dig the holes to a depth of about 24 inches. Clear all vegetation from the site. Spread a sheet of plastic over the site and cover it with a layer of gravel.

6 Steps or balustrade?

If the decking is higher than 8 inches off the ground, you will need steps. Most local councils have a building code that describes when a balustrade should be included (it is preferable if the decking is more than two steps high).

5 Cover with decking

Decking boards can be laid lengthwise, crosswise, or diagonally. The simplest method is to lay them at right angles to the joists, with board lengths selected at random, so end joints are staggered.

Set a board in place so that one end is centered on a joist, and then mark and cut the other end so that it centers on the nearest joist. Continue doing this across the frame.

4 Build the inner frame

Divide the length of the frame into 12-inch pieces. Cut the joists and fix to the beam frame with their centers at the 12-inch marks, aiming for a tight push-fit. Use nails, screws, or metal hangers. Fix a second row of joists to cross the width of the frame—these should be no more than 12 inches apart. There are many thoughts on joist size and spacing, but the smaller the lumber dimensions, the closer the spacing of posts and joists needs to be. If you are uncertain, ask the supplier for spacing specifications, to make sure the construction is safe.

2 Fix the posts

Put 8 inches of compacted hardpan into each hole. Sit the treated posts in position in the holes, propping them upright with temporary battens. Make checks with a carpenter's level. Fill the holes with concrete to just above ground level. Use a trowel to angle the top edge of the concrete, so that the slope will throw off the rain.

3 Build the beam frame

Cut and fit the beams to make an outer frame that runs from post to post. Tack the beams in place, check with the carpenter's level, and make adjustments. Secure the frame at each beam–post intersection with 3/4-inch-diameter stainless-steel nuts, bolts, and washers.

DECKING BOARD PATTERNS

Some people like plain decking, while others prefer a more complicated design. As a general rule, a pattern of decking boards uses more lumber and takes more time; however, the two parquet herringbone designs below show that an interesting pattern can be achieved simply by doubling up the joists at the point where the board ends are fixed.

Angled 45° to the run of the joists

Square-cut herringbone with doubled joists

Angle-cut zigzag with doubled joists

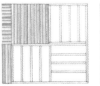
Large-module checkerboard parquet

Parallel to the house and at right angles to the joists

Single large diamond with doubled joists

Although designs involving a pattern of boards are expensive and time-consuming, you can speed up the work and keep wastage to a minimum simply by using a power miter saw (chop saw).

BALUSTRADE

If your decking patio is more than a couple of steps off the ground, you need to fit a balustrade (sometimes called a railing) for safety reasons. A balustrade will completely transform the look of the decking, making it more of a focal point.

A balustrade with integral posts, fretted boards, a top rail, and decorative finials.

It is possible to build a perfectly good add-on balustrade to a patio, with all the members fixed to the main ring beam or fascia, but it is best to consider the structure at the initial design stage. For example, in the design pictured above, the balustrade posts are simply an extension of the main support posts, giving a structure that is both stable and strong. Integral posts such as these are safer than an add-on option.

STEPS

If decking is more than 8 inches high, it will need steps (or one or more small decking platforms). Try to design steps to relate to the design of the balustrade. (See page 60.)

Maintenance

Sweep up debris and make sure that all parts of the structure are ventilated, so that the wood remains dry. (See page 41.)

Decorative patios

What is a decorative patio?

An area of concrete makes a perfectly good patio, which will be dry, firm and level. But if you stud the concrete with cobblestones, you will lift it from a merely functional structure to something altogether more decorative. If some part of a form has no reason for its existence other than to be pleasing to the eye, it can be defined as decorative. There are lots of ways to make a decorative patio by using various materials, patterns, planting, and ornaments.

THINGS TO CONSIDER

Pattern and style

↗ Select a pattern and style that complement the design and location of your home. Just as you might theme a room in the house in a certain color, and use particular shapes or forms, apply the same principles to the patio.

Feasibility

↗ Even if you are very keen on a certain type of material, it may not be feasible to use it for an entire patio, for example if the cost is prohibitive. If that is the case, consider using a small number of units within the design to create a feature.

Practicalities

↗ Above all else, a patio must be safe and comfortable underfoot. For example, large cobblestones are beautiful and hardwearing, but are they going to feel too lumpy? Glass is very attractive, but is it going to be dangerous for children?

DECORATIVE PATIO OPTIONS

Brick and stone combinations

↗ This is a classic, traditional mixture of old bricks and stone, perfect for an old house in the town or country. The bricks are ideal for patterning between the stones. Another idea is to leave out various stones, and use spaces as planting pockets. These look very effective when filled with low-growing rockery plants such as house leeks, thyme, and camomile.

Cut stone and pot plants

↗ A patio made from cut stone decorated with an infill of plants—ideal for a small city garden.

Decorative patterns

➜ An individualistic flourish can be added by combining materials. Here, stone blocks are cut to shape and arranged to form overlapping circles. The circle shapes are accentuated by infills of cobblestones pressed into the concrete.

Concrete and grass

↗ Plain concrete slabs decorated with ribbons of grass—an inexpensive option.

HOW TO MAKE A DECORATIVE PATIO USING CONCRETE SLABS

Choose a selection of concrete slabs, curbs, pavers, and stone blocks, all in the same muted color tone, and all much the same thickness.

Remove the grass and topsoil, and lay down a generous footing of compacted hardpan. Top with a slab of medium-strength concrete. Set the units on small blobs of mortar. Fill the joints with a dryish mix of mortar.

Step 4
When the mortar has set, brush and trowel a crumbly, dryish mix of mortar into the wide joints. Finally, spray the whole patio with a fine mist of water. Leave for at least 48 hours.

Step 3
Starting with the main design framework (the outer edge and the inner lozenge), set each slab on four or five small blobs of mortar. Adjust the thickness of the mortar to accommodate variations in the thickness of the different slabs and stone blocks. Leave generous joints between the slabs.

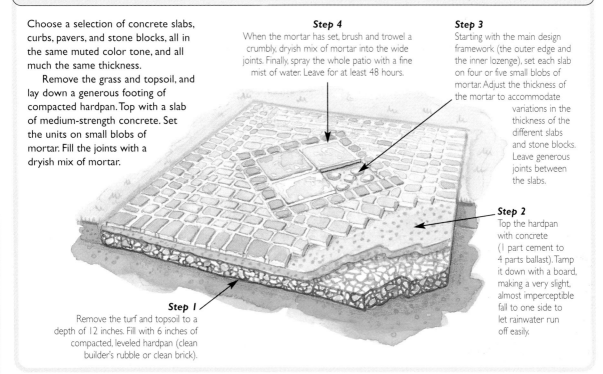

Step 2
Top the hardpan with concrete (1 part cement to 4 parts ballast). Tamp it down with a board, making a very slight, almost imperceptible fall to one side to let rainwater run off easily.

Step 1
Remove the turf and topsoil to a depth of 12 inches. Fill with 6 inches of compacted, leveled hardpan (clean builder's rubble or clean brick).

HOW TO MAKE A PATCHWORK SLATE MOSAIC PATIO

Step 3
Lay the pieces of slate (dry) and arrange them for best fit and decorative effect. Check lines and angles with a straight-edge and a set square. Use a piece of chalk to mark out a guide grid for laying the slate.

Step 4
Starting with the main elements of the design, bed the slate in mortar. Check each piece with a carpenter's level.

Step 5
When the mortar is dry and the slate is firm underfoot, fill the joints with a waterproof grout. Sponge grout off the surface of the slate.

✔ Start by selecting rectilinear pieces of real slate in different colors and textures. If possible, work out a design that avoids the need to cut the slate; if it is unavoidable, only make straight cuts. Lay down a hardpan footing topped with a concrete slab. Arrange the pieces of slate dry, spending time achieving the best fit. Finally, set the slate on a skim of mortar.

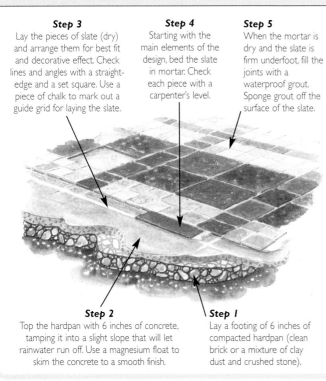

This alternative patchwork design consists of a mixture of slate and reconstituted stone, and incorporates an integral barbecue.

Step 2
Top the hardpan with 6 inches of concrete, tamping it into a slight slope that will let rainwater run off. Use a magnesium float to skim the concrete to a smooth finish.

Step 1
Lay a footing of 6 inches of compacted hardpan (clean brick or a mixture of clay dust and crushed stone).

Split-level patios

If your garden is sloping, covered with old concrete footings, or in any way less than level, you will need to create level areas if you want a place to sit, or somewhere for the children to play. One of the easiest ways of creating horizontal areas in a sloping garden is to build a split-level patio. Also, in a very flat and rather boring garden, a split-level patio can provide a high-rise "room," which gives exciting views across the garden.

EXAMPLES OF SPLIT-LEVEL PATIOS

↗ If you want to create a beautiful, long-lasting, traditional split-level patio, with steps, terraces, flagstones, random stone raised beds, and planting areas, real stone is the answer.
→ Bricks look equally good in a city backyard or in a cottage garden. They are easy to obtain, available in many different colors and textures, light to handle, and easy to work with.

↗ Decking is a great way of building a split-level patio. It doesn't require big footings or retaining walls: you simply build a series of platforms or steps at different levels.

SPLIT-LEVEL PATIO CONSTRUCTION DETAILS

→ When you are building a split-level patio in brick, you are in effect constructing one or more giant terraces or steps. If the ground is soft or crumbly, you need to build retaining walls to hold back the earth and to support the weight of the horizontal paving. All the walls need to be built on a traditional hardpan and concrete footing.

→ The walls of a split-level stone patio must be built on a hardpan and concrete footing. High walls (over 3 feet high) need to be buttressed to provide extra support (wider at the base than the top, with a vertical inside face and an angled outside face). Get professional help with this.

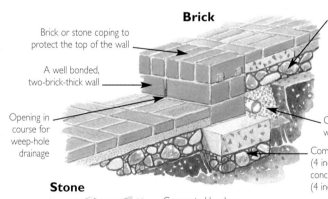

Brick

Brick or stone coping to protect the top of the wall

A well bonded, two-brick-thick wall

Opening in course for weep-hole drainage

Compacted hardpan (4 inches thick) and concrete footing slab (3 inches thick) under the brick pavers

Coarse backfill with drainage pipe

Compacted hardpan (4 inches thick) and concrete footing slab (4 inches thick)

Stone

Compacted hardpan (4 inches thick) and concrete footing slab (3 inches thick) under the paving slabs

Backfill of loose gravel for swift drainage

Concrete footing slab (4 inches thick) on 4 inches of compacted hardpan

Split-level decking

If you want to build a split-level patio without too much disturbance to the site, or if you enjoy working with wood, instead of brick or stone, or you want the job done fast, decking is the answer. (See pages 34–35.)

Circular patios

Primitive man thought that the circle was a magical symbol, and circular patios have a timeless quality that somehow makes them special. Perhaps it is the perfect symmetry of circles that makes them so attractive. They also provide an excellent opportunity for creating a pattern in different colors and materials, to make a striking motif. If you want to build a patio that makes an eye-catching feature, consider trying one of these.

Why choose a circular patio?

CIRCULAR PATIO OPTIONS

Paved circle	Decorative combination	Circle in a square or rectangle	Decking (and polygons)	More options
		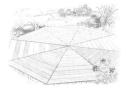		*You could make a cobblestoned circle with a millstone at its center, or a series of circular decking patios at different levels. A patio made entirely out of old bricks would be distinctive (however, this involves a lot of work and is quite difficult to build). (See page 9.)*
↗ *There are many circle-making pavers on the market—perfect for an instant patio.*	↗ *Bricks and stone blocks are a traditional combination, but there are many others.*	↗ *A round flagstone feature in a square patio makes an exciting geometrical mix.*	↗ *Not quite a circle, but a decking polygon (a hexagon or octagon) is the next best thing.*	

POSITIONING CIRCULAR PATIOS

Position a comfortable chair in a likely spot and relax with a cup of coffee. Does the site feel right? If so, mark out the circle with sand (see page 14) and see how it relates to the rest of the garden. Live with it for a few days before committing.

Sun and shade balance
Find a sheltered, sunny spot, with just the right amount of shade—perhaps from a nearby tree.

Sloping sites
If the site is steeply sloped, think about a split-level patio—perhaps a series of terraces or an area of raised decking with steps.

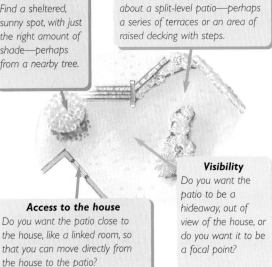

Visibility
Do you want the patio to be a hideaway, out of view of the house, or do you want it to be a focal point?

Access to the house
Do you want the patio close to the house, like a linked room, so that you can move directly from the house to the patio?

HOW TO BUILD A CIRCULAR CLEFT-STONE PAVING PATIO

→ ↘ Scribe out the circle (see page 14), and remove the turf and topsoil to a depth of 12 inches. Fill with 8 inches of compacted hardpan and top with 2 inches of sharp sand. Fit a small area (dry) so that you know how to place the pieces. Set the stones on a generous layer of a dryish mix of concrete. Point the gaps with mortar.

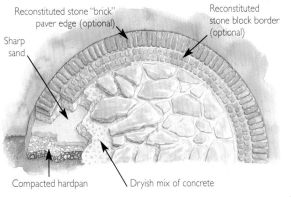

Reconstituted stone "brick" paver edge (optional)

Reconstituted stone block border (optional)

Sharp sand

Compacted hardpan

Dryish mix of concrete

Patio edgings

Why do patios need to be edged?

Patios need edging for three reasons: structure, decoration, and practicality. At the structural level, an edging contains a patio—without it, the patio would slowly ooze, spread, and self-destruct under its own weight. At the decorative level, an edging defines a patio, like a frame around a picture. At the practical level, an edging stops grass or flowers from invading a patio, making it easier to keep the garden neat and in good order.

WHAT IS A PATIO EDGING?

A patio edging can be anything from a row of bricks hidden away just below the surface of the ground, to a decorative wall complete with integral raised borders, pillars, seating, a barbecue, and planting.

The type you choose depends upon the size, site, and materials of the patio, but you also need to decide (at the design stage) whether the edging is to be a highly visible feature, or whether it can do its job hidden from view.

PATIO WALLS

A stone wall topped with slabs makes a beautiful, traditional edging that is handy for seating, or for displaying plants.

If you have the time and money, you can extend and enlarge an edging into a wall that can become a dynamic structure in its own right, such as a seat or a raised bed.

If your patio has a drop of two or more steps between it and the ground, it requires a safety barrier. You could build a wall that is both a balustrade to prevent you falling off, and a visually exciting decorative feature.

PATIO EDGING OPTIONS

Quick edgings

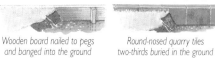

Wooden board nailed to pegs and banged into the ground

Round-nosed quarry tiles two-thirds buried in the ground

← and t small a in structure create a quick e simply by half-bury. bricks, wood, or tiles shallow trench.

Ready-made log roll strip, half-buried in the ground

Bricks set end to end and half-buried in the ground

Zigzag brick edgings

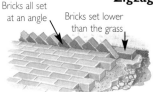

Bricks all set at an angle

Bricks set lower than the grass

← A row of zigzag bricks set at an angle in mortar, with a row of bricks set flat down to one side, makes the perfect edge between a patio and a lawn. Mowing is easy—a lawnmower can be pushed hard up against the zigzag bricks.

Mini brick wall edgings

→ This is the perfect edging when you want to create a strong division between the patio and the lawn. The wall is built on a concrete footing, and some part of the wall is buried below ground. The trench between the wall and the lawn is filled with gravel to hold back the lawn.

Trench filled with gravel

Brick wall on a concrete footing

Balustrading and safety

If you have a patio that is a couple of steps higher than a lawn, you can surround it with a decorative wall if you wish. However, if the patio is raised higher than 12 inches, a barrier is compulsory for safety reasons—the local building code would insist on a balustrade of at least waist height. If your site is exposed, you are worried about children's safety, or you want privacy, you can design the balustrade so that it doubles as a screen.

This wooden balustrade also acts as a screen around a raised patio.

Maintenance

It is no good walking out onto your patio on the first day of spring and expecting it to be in tip-top condition and ready to use, if you have ignored it since the summer. It will be covered in debris, the woodwork might well be green and slimy, and all the cracks and crannies will be full of bugs. A patio needs to be kept in order with a program of regular maintenance, with tasks to carry out before and after each season of patio use.

What does maintenance involve? Is it necessary?

BASIC PATIO MAINTENANCE

early spring, at the end of
and just

taining
patio. Also
the condition
ditions such as
rs, walls, trellises,
features, lighting
barbecues.

Concrete paver and slab maintenance

Removing weeds and moss
Don't let these invasive plants get a hold: remove them as soon as they appear. Dig out rather than using weedkiller.

Gap filling
Clean all the debris from the gaps and fill them either with silver sand or a dry, crumbly mortar made with fine sand and cement.

Efflorescence
There are four ways to tackle a patio that shows a white deposit called efflorescence: you can brush it off every time it appears, you can use a proprietary remover, you can wash it with vinegar, or you can leave it alone (it looks unsightly but is harmless).

Cleaning pavers
Sweep up debris and scrub with soapy water. Bleach or special cleaners, together with a hose or pressure spray, will help wash off algae.

Replacing broken pavers
If the paver is cracked, whack it with a hammer and use an old chisel to ease the fragments clear. Remove old mortar and debris from the recess. Check that the replacement paver is a good fit and then bed it in sand or mortar. Fill the joints to match.

MAINTAINING BRICKS AND CONCRETE PAVERS

Early every spring, brick and paver patios need a good wash and scrub. Use an old knife or chisel to scrape the joints clear of weeds and ants, and sweep up the debris. Scrub the surface with soapy water and mop dry. If the surface is green or slimy, add a small amount of bleach to the water. If you want a sheen or shiny finish to the surface, brush it with a proprietary finish or sealant.

MAINTAINING REAL STONE

Apart from regular brushing, a real stone patio is best left to develop a patina. If the patina presents a danger (for instance if the surface is breaking away, or it is slippery underfoot), you need to tackle it each season. Sweep up debris and mop down the patio with water containing a little bleach. Clean old and cracked mortar from the joints and repair with mortar (1 part cement, 6 parts soft sand, 1 part lime).

OTHER MAINTENANCE TIPS

The best single tip is to keep the patio well swept. On the face of it, this does not sound very efficacious, but the sweeping process both helps prevent trouble and reveals problems at an early stage. For example, it gets rid of piles of leaves, which might house vermin or become slippery underfoot, it disposes of ants' nests, and it discloses broken slabs and cracked mortar. If you discover a small problem after sweeping, sort it out before it gets bigger and more difficult to remedy.

MAINTAINING DECKING PATIOS

If wooden decking is sturdily built and well looked after and maintained, it will last about 25 years. The biggest danger is damp. If the wood is well ventilated, it doesn't matter if it gets soaked when it rains, then dries out in the sun and wind, but if it is constantly damp, the wood will soon break down under insect attack and various molds. The best defense is to sweep up debris, remove algae with soap and water, and then let the decking dry. Do this in spring and the fall.

If existing decking is a poor, softwood construction, the best thing to do is to protect it with garden paint. (If you are about to build some decking, either use a top-quality hardwood, or a special pressure-treated softwood.)

Revitalizing existing patios

Can I do anything about my terrible patio?

Most patios can be reborn if you lavish a little time, money, and effort on them. Small patios can be enlarged, ugly concrete patios can be covered over, cracked concrete pavers can be lifted and replaced, old bricks can be enhanced, boring patios can be embellished with features and planting or kitted out with new furniture, and so on. If you are fed up with your existing patio, it can definitely be given a facelift.

HOW TO TRANSFORM A DULL PATIO

BEFORE

WHAT MAKES A PATIO LOOK DULL?

If a patio is uninspiring, it is often due to neglect. Old plastic furniture is pushed to one side, broken pots are left in corners, weeds are allowed to grow through it, and so on. Once a patio becomes a dumping ground, nobody will want to use it—sitting outside in an unloved area, surrounded by junk, is unappealing. But a patio that gets lots of use is never dull—the seats are comfortable and dry, and it is generally an attractive place where people want to spend time. (See patio maintenance on page 41.)

Furniture

Choose comfortable patio furniture: chairs or a bench and perhaps sun loungers. You will also need a table. If you don't want to have to bring furniture indoors when it rains, select the material accordingly. (See page 64.)

Planting

Just as you might embellish a room in your home with pictures on the wall and drapes at the windows, a garden room —your patio—benefits from being embellished with plants. Groups of ferns around a water feature, a collection of bonsai trees, a raised bed planted with graceful grasses, one or more really spectacular plants—there are lots of possibilities. If your patio is slightly sheltered, it can be used as a nursery area for seedlings. (See page 68.)

Type of surface

There is nothing quite so dull and depressing as a bald patch of gray concrete. It will last forever, but after a year or two you might very well begin to wish that it would just go away. But then again, concrete makes a perfect base for bricks. Genuine rustic bricks look great and are particularly good in a country garden. If the bricks are old and slightly bruised at the corners, so much the better. (See page 32.)

AFTER

Lighting

Nothing improves a patio more quickly than low-level spotlights positioned to pick out special features. (See page 79.)

Water features

There is something rather comforting about sitting on a patio and enjoying the sights and sounds of moving water. A water feature doesn't have to be anything large or dramatic—a small waterspout set in a wall, gently bubbling and splashing into a pool, is ideal and something that children can safely enjoy. (See page 77.)

Ornaments and sculpture

A sculpture or ornament will liven up a dull corner—perhaps a ceramic cat, a boot scraper doorstop, a gnome, a collection of ceramic tiles, or some old tools. (See page 72.)

The addition of an arbor provides some privacy and shade, as well as giving a new dimension to a straightforward patio. A large, striking urn injects drama.

EXTENDING A PATIO

Extending a paved area

There is no reason why a patio cannot be extended on one or all sides. It is better not to try and match the existing materials, because products change in size and style over the years, but rather to look at it as a chance to brighten up the whole patio by framing it with new and exciting materials.

For example, you could frame an existing concrete paver patio with bricks, real stone, or concrete slabs in a different color. Measure the existing patio, decide on the preferred size of the units, bricks or slabs, and then search out new materials that fit into this scheme.

More unusual ways of extending a paved area

← An existing patio can be slowly extended by making gradual additions to the sides. First, for example, you could add a small area of concrete studded with cobblestones. This might be supplemented by some roundel (circular) slabs and more cobblestones interspersed with planting.

Extending decking

→ Wooden decking can be extended by building another deck at one side. To add interest, do not build it on the same level and to the same shape. Instead, alter the shape, skew it slightly, and make it several steps higher. A small platform will make a step between the two.

IS THE PATIO IN THE WRONG PLACE?

Over time, things change—trees grow taller, neighbors might build an intrusive extension that cuts out the sunlight, a road might become bigger and noisier, and so on—all factors that might spoil your enjoyment of a once-comfortable patio. If this happens, consider all the possibilities. Would it be sensible to move the patio slightly and reuse part of the old footing? Could you lift the whole thing and reuse all the materials? If you built a screen to one side to add privacy or to protect you from an obtrusive view, would it improve matters? Could you prune a tree to let in more sunlight?

If none of these options is feasible, the existing patio is too small and not quite in the right place, or you have moved to a new house and you don't like the patio, you might as well write it off and start over again. However, don't be in too much of a hurry to do this, because there is always the chance that with a lot of lateral thinking, other possibilities will present themselves.

Before you remove an old patio, consider whether it could be used for a new purpose, such as a children's play area, or as a base for a new workshop. If the materials cannot be reclaimed intact, perhaps they can be put to good use as hardpan.

REUSING A FOOTING

If you like the position of your patio and are only going to increase its size slightly, there is no reason why you cannot reuse part of the old footing. All you do is lay an additional concrete slab to the side of the original one, and build the patio extension.

COVERING A PATIO

Sometimes a patio is perfectly positioned and just the right size, but not very attractive to look at. If this is the case, simply cover it over with a new material. Remove all the features and materials that are worth saving, and make good the patio surface with extra concrete. Build the surrounding edging slightly higher, and then cover the whole patio with bricks or decking. (See pages 32–35.)

Choosing paths and steps

Paths look fairly easy; are steps difficult to do?

Most beginners are happy enough building paths and wooden steps, but are worried about the prospect of building a flight of traditional steps (such as a run of three brick steps), often because they cannot visualize or understand the order of work. Steps are built from the bottom tread upward. In essence, all you do is build a series of little platforms, with each successive platform or tread raised and offset from its neighbor.

OPTIONS FOR PATHS AND STEPS

Gravel and logs	Stone	Decorative	Wooden	Brick and tile

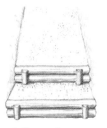    

↑ *The perfect steps for a country garden: logs or risers set the height of the steps and create a feature, and compacted fine gravel is used for the treads.*

↑ *Traditional stone steps made from a mixture of cut stone for the risers, step nosings and side walls, and cleft-stone paving for the treads.*

↑ *A beautiful flight of courtyard steps, with terra-cotta tiles for both risers and treads. These steps would look great in a small, walled town garden.*

↑ *A flight of steps made entirely from reclaimed railroad ties—a long-lasting, easy-to-build option, suitable for a country or city garden.*

↑ *Traditional brick and tile steps. The bricks are set on edge to make the risers, and tiles are used to make a decorative feature out of the treads.*

PLANNING PATHS AND STEPS IN THE GARDEN

A formal garden layout (plan view)

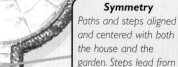
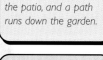

Straight lines
As far as possible, the paths run in straight lines parallel to the sides of the garden. There are no wandering curves or free bends.

Symmetry
Paths and steps aligned and centered with both the house and the garden. Steps lead from the patio, and a path runs down the garden.

Geometry
If the path needs to change direction, it must do so at right angles, using squares or circles at important junctions.

Pattern
Subtle patterns created in traditional materials (stone, bricks, tiles and cobblestones), not brightly colored tiles or paint.

An informal garden layout (plan view)

↗ Try to foster the impression that the garden has been created over many years. Avoid drawing formal plans, stay away from designs that are geometric and symmetrical, and generally let designs evolve to suit changing needs. Encourage paths to meander around the garden, just as people might wander from one area to another.

Quick paths and steps

I t is quite possible to make a path and a flight of steps in the space of a couple of weekends, by spending the first weekend planning the operation, and the second building. It will be hard work: the building weekend will involve long days, and you will need help, but provided that there is good weather, it is possible to complete a project in this timespan. Some of the more complicated projects may require a little concrete.

Can I build quickly without a lot of concrete?

QUICK PATHS

Gravel
➜ *A gravel path is quick to make. Clear the turf and topsoil, spread 4 inches of compacted hardpan, cover with woven weed-stop plastic, and top with 4 inches of gravel. Edge the path with large rocks.*

Stepping stones
➜ *Stepping stones are great for an informal garden. Dig out the turf, bed the stones on sand.*
➘ *You can create an instant, winding path with decking "stepping stones"—remove the turf and set the circles in place.*

Wooden walkway
➘ *Wooden walkways suit a country garden and also make a fine path to complement decking. Use pressure-treated wood. To make a walkway, put two parallel wooden rails directly on the ground and nail boards in place across them. If the site is wet, you can set the rails on concrete blocks.*

More ideas
• Try a path made from salvaged sturdy poles, boards, and gravel (illustrated right).
• Crushed tree bark makes an instant, biodegradable path, which is perfect for a traditional country cottage garden.
• A mixture of crushed stone and sharp sand makes an instant path.

QUICK STEPS

Post and bark
➜ *Log posts, pegged in place, define the width of the steps; thicker logs decide step height and the spacing of the treads. The treads are lined with plastic and topped with bark or gravel.*

Wooden plank steps
➜ *Traditional steps with open risers, side boards, and plank treads. All the joints can be made using metal angle plates—a really good option for porch steps or steps leading to an area of decking.*

Decking steps
➜ *Broad decking steps can be built to cover existing steps—useful for improving mean, narrow steps, or when you want to build wide steps to give easy and safe access for children or older people.*

More ideas
• You could build a flight of steps using concrete blocks stacked and mortared together, and then rendered.
• You could look for a steps "kit" in a reclamation yard: part of an old cast-iron fire escape or spiral staircase.
• Logs and planks make good steps.
• A series of wooden platforms, at slightly different heights and set side by side, would make shallow steps.
• Stacked concrete blocks, mortared together, with reconstituted stone slabs on top, make sturdy steps.

Basic paths

How do I make a path from house to patio?

Some people live in a house for years, continually wishing that they had paths running to the lawn, vegetable garden, or patio, and yet they don't do anything about it because they think that paths are complex structures to build. However, there are lots of ways to create a basic path, some of which are very simple. The process does not even have to involve lots of heavy digging—gravel or stepping stones are two very uncomplicated options.

IDEAS FOR BASIC PATHS

Gravel path	Concrete path	Brick path	Stepping-stone path

A traditional path made from fine gravel—its crunchy texture is enjoyable to walk on.

Concrete paths are straightforward to make and can last for hundreds of years.

A traditional red brick path laid in a herringbone pattern—perfect for a cottage garden.

Large, weathered slabs of real stone make delightful stepping stones across a lawn.

A GRAVEL PATH

A path made from fine gravel is one of the easiest types of path to lay, and the sound of gravel underfoot is a joy. Remove the turf, dig down to a depth of about 8 inches, edge the path with boards, spread a layer of compacted hardpan and top this with gravel. If the ground is dry, just remove the turf, put down a sheet of woven weed-stop plastic and spread the gravel.

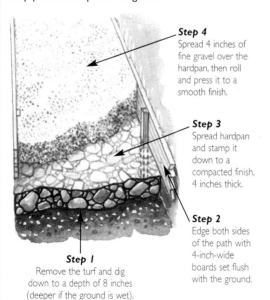

Step 4
Spread 4 inches of fine gravel over the hardpan, then roll and press it to a smooth finish.

Step 3
Spread hardpan and stamp it down to a compacted finish, 4 inches thick.

Step 2
Edge both sides of the path with 4-inch-wide boards set flush with the ground.

Step 1
Remove the turf and dig down to a depth of 8 inches (deeper if the ground is wet).

A CONCRETE PATH

A narrow, straight-as-an-arrow concrete path is very appealing in its simplicity. First, remove the turf and dig down to a depth of about 8 inches. Edge the path with a a board, spread 4 inches of compacted hardpan, and top it with 4 inches of tamped concrete.

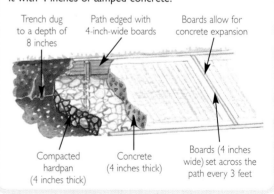

Trench dug to a depth of 8 inches

Path edged with 4-inch-wide boards

Boards allow for concrete expansion

Compacted hardpan (4 inches thick)

Concrete (4 inches thick)

Boards (4 inches wide) set across the path every 3 feet

MORE BASIC PATHS

A path can be as basic as you wish—for example, stepping stones, crushed stone, shingle, crushed shell, crushed tree bark, concrete blocks, cobblestones, or pebbles embedded in mortar. If you can come up with a material that is long-lasting and firm, dry, and nonslippery underfoot, it will serve as a path. If the ground is hard, you can build straight on top of it, but if it is wet, you need to remove the turf and topsoil, lay and compact hardpan, and stop the path from spreading by edging it with boards or bricks.

Natural paths

Anatural path is a more informal type of path that attempts to recreate a look from nature. At heart, it is a strip of more or less level land that is dry and comfortable underfoot—and by replicating woody, stony, shingly, or sandy conditions, you can build a path that perhaps paints a picture of hiking through mountains, exploring a mysterious forest, pottering around a seaside haunt, or crossing imposing desert scenery.

How do I make a path that doesn't look man-made?

Stepping stones casually meander across a sea of fine gravel planted with species that enjoy well-drained conditions, such as rock plants, grasses, and plants of Mediterranean origin.

CHOOSING A THEME

Once you have decided to build a natural path, you need to analyze which features define your chosen example. For instance, a real shoreline beach path is made up of pebbles and sand, and there may be larger water-washed stones and scattered pieces of driftwood lying about. These characteristics need to be incorporated into your design, so that they instantly transport the path user to that environment.

CHOOSE A PRACTICAL OPTION

Try to match the envisaged path to your existing garden. You might want a beach path, but if your garden is damp, with a clay soil and lush plants, and a dense tree canopy, a beach path might look rather out of place.

MAINTENANCE

A natural path will, to a greater or lesser extent, need regular maintenance—leaves removing, topping up with pebbles or bark, the edges tending, and so on—just like any other path.

HOW TO CREATE A NATURAL-LOOKING WOODLAND PATH

The characteristics of a woodland path are that it is dry and soft underfoot, and snakes around trees, wet areas, and the occasional rock or fallen tree, with the width of the path changing to suit the terrain.

Look at your garden and find the best way of routing the path to take in existing features, such as a pond or trees. Use pegs and string to mark out the route. Clear the turf and remove the soil to a depth of about 8 inches. Put 4 inches of compacted hardpan in the trench and top it with a sheet of woven weed-stop plastic. Cover this with a mixture of crushed bark, wood chips, and leaf mold. Position feature rocks at the side, plus a large log or tree trunk that is big enough to sit on. Plant ferns, bluebells, bushes, and scrub trees on both sides of the path.

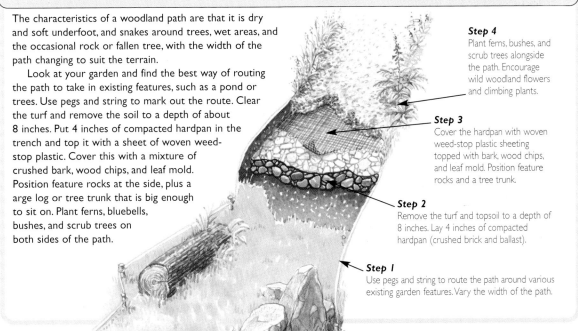

Step 4
Plant ferns, bushes, and scrub trees alongside the path. Encourage wild woodland flowers and climbing plants.

Step 3
Cover the hardpan with woven weed-stop plastic sheeting topped with bark, wood chips, and leaf mold. Position feature rocks and a tree trunk.

Step 2
Remove the turf and topsoil to a depth of 8 inches. Lay 4 inches of compacted hardpan (crushed brick and ballast).

Step 1
Use pegs and string to route the path around various existing garden features. Vary the width of the path.

Brick or paver paths

Brick paths are time-consuming to make, but not difficult. After removing turf and topsoil from the site and completing the basic structures as for any other path, you are faced with the task of laying the bricks. However, in their favor, bricks are handy and comfortable to work with, there is something uniquely interesting about the way they fit together, and at the end of the project you will have a path that lasts a lifetime.

A basketweave brick path makes an attractive, practical division between flower borders, and is a particularly good option for a cottage garden.

A wide brick path provides a useful dry area between the house and garden, and allows easy mowing of the lawn. Its width means there is enough space for substantial planters.

A diagonal herringbone path bordered by cobblestones set in mortar. Clay pavers have been selected in a range of colors to give an interesting twist to a traditional design.

TYPES OF CLAY BRICK

For garden projects, it is best to use well-fired (or high-fired) exterior-grade bricks, or engineering bricks, both of which are harder than standard bricks, with low rates of water absorption and good frost resistance. Reclaimed bricks may be available from an architectural salvage company.

Avoid new bricks manufactured to look like old—the decorative face will abrade if used on a path, and they can only be used stretcher face uppermost.

New engineering brick— good for edgings

Old worn and weathered high-fired brick

BLOCK PAVERS

Pavers (or paviors) are extremely hard, thin clay or concrete bricks designed specifically for paths, patios, and drives. They come in many shapes, sizes, and finishes. Perhaps the most attractive and durable option is the kiln-fired, brick-sized clay paver, in subtle colors that never fade. Concrete pavers include imitation stone "setts" (small rectangular paving blocks) and mock bricks.

Genuine kiln-fired clay paver

Concrete pavers imitating stone "setts"

BRICK PATH CONSIDERATIONS

Bricks have two end or "header" faces, two side or "stretcher" faces, a top or "frog" face, and a bottom face. The pattern bricks are laid in is termed the bond. Consider how path style will affect costs.

Style ~ Brick paths are straight or gently curved, with bricks set frog face down or on their side (stretcher). Straight, narrow paths use the fewest bricks. Curved paths require bricks to be set on their side, so using more bricks and increasing costs.

Cost ~ You can cut costs by using concrete "brick" pavers, but these are a poor second to genuine clay bricks.

Number of cut bricks ~ Minimize costs and effort with a design that uses whole bricks rather than involving cutting.

Calculating brick quantities

1. Calculate the area ~ Measure the length and width of the path and multiply together to give the area.

2. Calculate the number of bricks ~ There are roughly 36 bricks to a square yard, so multiply the area by 36.

3. Add 5% for wastage ~ If you go for a design that uses whole bricks and you are careful, you can allow for about 5% wastage (if you reckon that you need 100 bricks, get 105).

PATTERNS FOR PATHS

There are two differences between clay bricks and concrete or clay pavers. Bricks can be laid with any face uppermost, but pavers can only be laid with the wide face uppermost. Also, brick sizes allow for wide joints, while pavers are designed to touch each other. Visit a builders' yard to buy the bricks or pavers, laying out a few on the ground in the desired pattern to see how they look.

Mitered herringbone

↗ *Clay pavers laid in a traditional herringbone; mitered where they meet the edging. A tricky pattern with lots of cutting.*

Square herringbone

↗ *Clay pavers laid in a traditional square herringbone pattern that only requires bricks to be cut in half.*

Face-up basketweave

↗ *Bricks laid face up in a 3-by-3 basketweave pattern. This attractive, traditional design has no bricks to cut.*

Frog-down basketweave

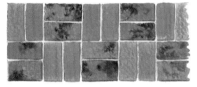

↗ *Bricks laid frog face down in a 2-by-2 basketweave pattern that uses fewer bricks, has no bricks to cut, but is not so subtle.*

TURNING CORNERS

With brick or paver paths, corners are best turned at right angles, so that your chosen pattern can be interlocked at the turn. This herringbone pattern is turned simply by following through in a different direction, and there is no need to cut many bricks.

HOW TO MAKE A BRICK PATH

Mark out the route and width of the path. Remove the turf and topsoil to a depth of 8 inches. Edge the path with wooden boards. Lay 3½ inches of compacted hardpan. Set the edge bricks in mortar. Lay ¾ inch of compacted ballast, ¾ inch of compacted sharp sand and a thin layer of raked soft sand. Position the bricks, brush fine sand into the joints, and use a plate compacter to compact them level.

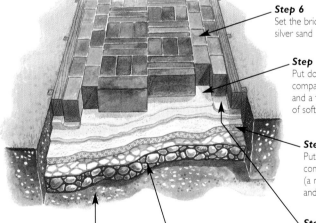

Step 6
Set the bricks in place. Brush silver sand into the joints.

Step 5
Put down ¾ inch of compacted sharp sand, and a thin layer (¼ inch) of soft sand.

Step 4
Put down ¾ inch of compacted ballast (a mixture of sand and gravel).

Step 3
Mortar a row of bricks along each edge, so that it is level with the boards.

Step 2
Put down a 3½-inch-thick layer of compacted hardpan (clean brick is best).

Step 1
Remove the turf and topsoil to a depth of 8 inches. Edge the path with boards set level.

CUTTING BRICKS

There are four ways of cutting a brick: you can give it a sharp blow with a stonemason's hammer, use a brick hammer with a brick chisel, get hold of an angle grinder, or rent a brick cutter (like a guillotine).

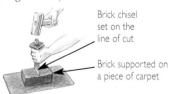

Brick chisel set on the line of cut

Brick supported on a piece of carpet

To use a brick chisel and stonemason's hammer, set the chisel on the mark and give it several crisp blows with the hammer.

CUTS TO AVOID

It is easier to cut a brick in half along its length (so that you finish up with two half bricks) than it is to cut at an angle. If you make lots of mistakes trying to cut bricks at an angle, the project is going to work out to be more expensive (in time and money) than intended. For these two very good reasons, it is best for beginners to choose a pattern that minimizes the need to cut bricks.

Decorative paths

Should I make a decorative path?

A path is primarily a utilitarian surface, but with added decoration, it can move beyond the merely functional. Designs can incorporate beautiful colors and textures, reveal patterns built up from the placement of various materials, or display motifs (reflecting a variety of imagery) stamped into concrete. The decoration can be in the edging or even the very shape of the path. The options for creativity are as broad as your imagination.

DESIGN AND INSPIRATION

Having first decided on the route of the path and its primary function, you need to look at what you can afford.

Let's say that you want a path to run from the back door of the house into the garden. It needs to be hardwearing and traditional. A red brick path laid out according to a traditional pattern is one solution. If, however, you would prefer a cheaper option, a gravel path with an edging made from salvaged bricks might be more appropriate.

Look at your house and garden, take into account your likes and dislikes, such as an antipathy for straight lines or a love of swirling patterns, and then draw inspiration from the color and texture of the site.

A path made from reconstituted stone slabs framed with cast "Celtic" pavers. There are many such pavers on the market.

Questions to ask yourself

Assess the purpose ~ Is the path to be purely functional—for example, to go around the vegetables? Or is it to make a design statement in the garden? Select materials accordingly.

Choose an appropriate style ~ A path made from railroad ties might look good in a country garden, but how would it look in your city courtyard? Consider the proportion of the units in relation to their surroundings.

Think about the cost ~ Gravel is the cheapest and real stone flagstones are the most expensive. How much do you want to spend? Is money an issue?

Consider curves and bends ~ Curvy and winding paths are best made from small components such as gravel and bricks, which give flexibility in design.

SOME CLASSIC DECORATIVE PATH DESIGNS

DECORATIVE BRICK PATHS

Brick paths are one of the most traditional and the most flexible in design terms. In many ways, they are also the easiest to lay. Special engineering bricks or well-fired house bricks are used, which are harder than regular bricks and will not crumble. (See page 48.)

Cleft-stone paving path

A traditional cleft-stone paving path. Randomly shaped pieces of stone are set in mortar on a footing of compacted hardpan.

Cobblestone path

A cobblestone path with a single line of bricks on either edge. The cobblestones are evenly spaced and pressed into mortar.

HOW TO MAKE A DECORATIVE PAVER PATH

→ ↘ Today we have the choice of using pavers (or paviors) to make a path, rather than following the traditional method of using engineering bricks, well-fired house bricks, or salvaged bricks. Pavers are super-hard, thin bricks made from clay or concrete, which are specifically for use in the construction of paths, drives, and patios. They come in many shapes and sizes, and various finishes—everything from simple brick lookalikes to imitation stone. The path illustrated uses two types of paver: "brick" stone blocks and "stone" tiles.

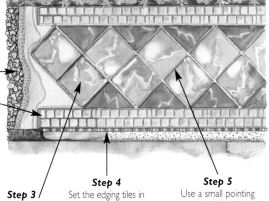

Step 1
Dig to a depth of 6 inches and fill with 2½ inches of compacted hardpan. Cover with 2 inches of concrete.

Step 2
Bed the border paver stone blocks on mortar, ensuring that they are level and flush with the ground at the side of the path.

Step 3
Cut and fit the tile pavers and bed them in mortar— so that they are level and flush with the border paver stone blocks.

Step 4
Set the edging tiles in place on mortar. Dig a slot trench and fill it with fine gravel (so that you can mow right up to the edge of the path).

Step 5
Use a small pointing trowel to fill the joints with a dryish mix of mortar. Carefully wipe the path clear of debris.

TEXTURAL PATTERN PATHS

A textural pattern takes its starting point from the character of the stone and evolves through the way the pieces of stone are laid down. Various textures of stone can be used to complement each other, or laid down in contrasting adjacent areas to underline the qualities of each material. From cleft stone to square slabs, cobblestones, or gravel, there are hundreds of options. Visit a builders' supplier for inspiration, then use your imagination to create an effective design.

Random slabs laid square to each other, with the joints filled with gravel.

Stone blocks placed in a traditional, structured shell design.

Granite blocks laid side by side according to best fit, in a traditional design.

BRICKS AND BLOCKS

Traditional bricks are usually about twice the thickness of modern stone paver blocks. If you want to mix the two to create a path, first lay the bricks in sand and then lay the blocks. In the illustration below, the joints have been planted with grass seed so that grass will bind the bricks and blocks together. The mower can be run straight over a path like this.

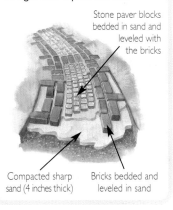

Stone paver blocks bedded in sand and leveled with the bricks

Compacted sharp sand (4 inches thick)

Bricks bedded and leveled in sand

COPING WITH CURVES

The trick to building a curved path is to use small units. The smaller the unit, the easier it is to create a curve. For example, a tight curve can be created by using small stone blocks, or broken half-bricks positioned best end uppermost.

PROBLEMS WITH LEVELS

Before starting a project, decide what level you want the finished path to be. Do you want it to be flush with the surrounding ground, or at a higher level than it? Dig the footing to suit. Adjust the depth of the hardpan according to the desired results.

BE CREATIVE WITH A MOSAIC PATH

A mosaic path will provide an artistic challenge. You need a firm footing consisting of 6 inches of compacted hardpan topped off with 3½ inches of concrete. If you are using broken tiles and crockery (all more or less the same thickness), use waterproof cement to bed them in place, which is less porous and gives better adhesion.

Curved paths

I would like a curved path—are they complicated?

Ameandering path with curvaceous bends is a wonderful sight. The complexity of the path depends on the materials used to build it. There is an old adage that says "spacing and placing is better than cutting"—it is much better to use materials that can be carefully spaced and placed to follow the line of the path, rather than to use a rigid grid of concrete slabs, for example, where the edge slabs need to be cut to fit the edge of the path.

SWEEPING CURVES

If the curve is big enough—for example, a sweeping curve running over a distance of 20 yards—it can almost be treated like a straight line. Wood edging can be bent into position, even the joints in brick and slab paths can be eased, tweaked and angled so that the path runs round the curve. Never try cutting large numbers of slabs to fit the curve—it's a difficult task, and the resulting path will look lifeless.

PROBLEMS WITH CURVES

When using materials such as slabs and blocks to build a curved path, the tighter the curve involved, the greater the problems presented. You have two choices if you must build a tightly curved path: either use materials that can easily run around curves, such as bark, concrete, gravel, small pavers, cobblestones set in concrete, or mosaic; or build it from thin materials such as slate, tiles, or old bricks, which can be set on edge and fanned out so that they readily run around both convex and concave curves.

The sweeping curve of this path is so broad that it can be achieved by adjusting the mortar joints between the bricks, letting them run smoothly around the curve.

Choosing materials for building curved paths

Path-building materials under consideration for a curved path can be divided into three categories, according to degree of complexity. When using fixed modular materials such as bricks or slabs, the challenge is to make the path's surface appear to flex with the curves.

Easy

Spread materials can be poured and raked, providing a very easy solution.

Fine gravel ~ Fine gravel is a good, traditional option—just rake and roll it over a base of hardpan. (See page 45.)

Crushed stone ~ Crushed stone can be treated in the same way as gravel.

Concrete ~ Concrete is a reliable option, especially if interest is added to the surface by patterning it with a brush, or studding with small pebbles.

Tree bark ~ Very easy to spread, firm underfoot and toddler-friendly. It can be put on the vegetable garden when it eventually breaks down.

Slightly more complex

The smaller the units chosen, the easier it makes the task.

Bricks ~ Old bricks, set on edge, can be arranged to fan around a curve. A very useful way of doing an edging.

Slate roof tiles ~ Broken roof tiles can be set in mortar so that only the edge is on show. For a traditional checkerboard design, slices of slate are grouped and bedded in mortar in this way. Slates look especially good in combination with brick.

Cobblestones ~ These are fun to use. They need a footing of compacted hardpan; mortar is spread on top and the cobblestones bedded in place.

To be avoided

Stay away from large modules, because they are very difficult to lay.

Square slabs ~ The only easy way to use these is to set them down like stepping stones, and surround them with a material such as gravel.

Railroad ties ~ These are heavy and difficult to cut—not really suitable for an average narrow garden path.

Ceramic tiles ~ Ceramic tiles are best avoided unless you want to break them up and create a mosaic path.

Shaped concrete slabs ~ Shaped slabs, such as hexagons, don't easily lend themselves to curves and tend to look out of place.

Path edgings

A path edging has both an esthetic and practical purpose. It trims the path, making it look crisply defined, structured, and pleasing to the eye. Much more importantly, the edging is a structural control that stops the path from spreading under its own weight and that of people using the path. Without a good edging, the sides of the path would erode, the lawn and weeds would creep in, and the whole path would gradually spread and sag in the center.

Do paths always need edgings?

PATH EDGE OPTIONS

In general, the best edgings are made from small units that can be spaced to fit around curves. They should be chosen to blend in with the overall character of the path and its setting.

Soldier bricks

These are perfect for straight or curved, formal or informal paths in brick, stone or gravel.

Angled bricks

Angled bricks are good for a path alongside a flowerbed, to keep earth off the path.

Decorative tiles

These look good with bricks, stone blocks, but terrible with natural materials like bark.

Log roll

Log-roll edging is ideal for meandering natural paths on uneven ground.

PATH EDGING EXAMPLES

Soldier bricks
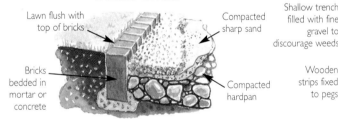

Lawn flush with top of bricks
Compacted sharp sand
Bricks bedded in mortar or concrete
Compacted hardpan

↗ Soldier bricks are set with the stretcher (side) face upright. This path of gravel over hardpan has the lawn flush with the top of the bricks to make mowing easy.

Wooden boards

Shallow trench filled with fine gravel to discourage weeds
Tamped concrete
Wooden strips fixed to pegs
Compacted hardpan

↗ Wooden boards are fixed to pegs to edge this concrete path. The lawn is at a lower level, with a shallow, gravel-filled trench between the lawn and the boards.

Victorian tiles
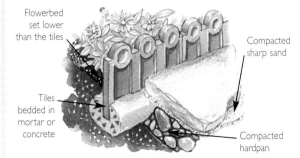

Flowerbed set lower than the tiles
Compacted sharp sand
Tiles bedded in mortar or concrete
Compacted hardpan

↗ These decorative tiles form an attractive edging, shown here on a path of slabs. The flowerbed is set lower than the path, so that the tile edging is on show. For best effect, use kiln-fired clay tiles rather than concrete.

PATH EDGING NOTES

Qualities of a good edging ~ All edgings need to be constructed in such a way that the path is well supported, but the definition of what constitutes a good edging changes according to the character of the path. For example, a good decorative edging would be one that is clearly on show, but a good edging for a natural path would be one that is hidden from view.

Things to avoid ~ Put decorative edgings on paths bordered by flowerbeds, rather than lawn, so that you are less likely to trip over them.

The necessity of edging ~ Some paths look best when the edge is hidden from view, like a meandering natural path made of bark, but all paths benefit from an edging. A concrete path is perhaps the only exception, and even then it needs a wooden edge during the time it is being cast.

Steps in paths

Can I have steps in my sloping garden path?

Unless your garden is as flat as a pancake, there will be places where you can include one or more steps. As well as paths, the possibilities include a sunken patio complete with steps, steps from the garden up to the patio, or from the patio down to the path. For a much grander scheme, turn the whole garden into a series of level terraces, perhaps with a patio by the house, a couple of flower borders, and steps running from one level to another.

SIMPLE STEPS IN PATHS

There are two options: dig steps into the slope of the ground, so that the sides are hidden from view, or build steps up from the slope so that the sides are on full view.

The first option is the easiest to build. The simplest steps—no more difficult than stacking children's building blocks—are those where the units that make up the steps become both the riser and the tread, as is the case when you use railroad ties.

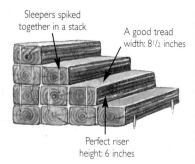

Sleepers spiked together in a stack

A good tread width: 8½ inches

Perfect riser height: 6 inches

A flight of steps made from 36-inch-long pieces of railroad ties. The 6-inch thickness becomes the height of the riser.

Would it be better to have a slope than steps?

You may prefer not to have steps if some garden users are not very agile, or so that a mower, wheelbarrow, or wheelchair can move unhindered. If the slope of the garden is gentle, there are other options.

Tree bark ~ A gently ascending slope of crushed tree bark is firm and dry underfoot, and easy to maintain.

Tamped concrete ~ The tamp marks in a long, sloping path of tamped concrete provide a good foothold.

STEPS IN NATURAL PATHS

Simple steps can be created by fixing logs across the width of a path and then spreading material (such as bark or gravel) behind them to make level areas, which become the treads. The logs become both the riser and the nosing to the treads. This design is very easy to build. To create a more architectural look, use railroad ties instead of logs.

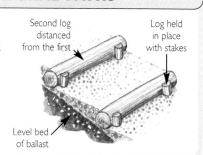

Second log distanced from the first

Log held in place with stakes

Level bed of ballast

CORNER STEPS IN A PATH

When building an angled turn in a flight of steps—say, where a path changes direction as it climbs up a slope—the simplest thing to do is create a "quarter dog-leg turn." In effect, this is a single square step that lets you turn comfortably in readiness for climbing onto the next step. If the steps are 36 inches wide, the square step would measure 36 x 36 inches.

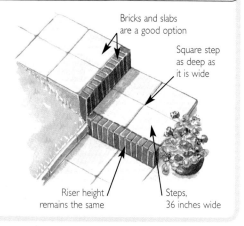

Bricks and slabs are a good option

Square step as deep as it is wide

Riser height remains the same

Steps, 36 inches wide

SAFETY CONSIDERATIONS

Seek professional advice and help if the flight of steps numbers greater than six, or if the ground is in any way unstable—such as very sandy, waterlogged, steep and rocky, or steep and crumbly, or if the land has been been reclaimed.

Steps are inherently very dangerous—older people may slip on them and children may stumble and roll down them—so it is vital to do your best to make sure that they are as safe as possible. If the steps are steep, incorporate handrails. Make sure that the treads are not slippery—do not make them from materials such as polished slate or wood that is liable to get green and slimy. Always keep the riser height constant (and no more than 4–6 inches) to avoid a situation where an unforeseen change to the rhythm of ascent or descent might catch someone unawares and cause him or her to lurch and trip.

Path solutions

The most obvious function of a garden path is as a direct walkway between two points, which takes the shortest route. A mixture of practical necessity, with a dash of decoration thrown in for good measure, successfully fulfils this garden role. Some paths are intended more as unhurried routes around the best features and views in the garden, and these may have a more decorative component to add to the enjoyment of the garden experience.

What is most important in a path?

This path circles a large country house. The border of bumpy cobblestones helps persuade visitors to keep to the path.

PRACTICAL PATHS

A good, practical path has to enable you to get from A to B without getting your feet wet. It needs to be firm and dry underfoot, with no slime or puddles, and it should get you to your destination quickly. Practical paths tend to be straight, and a decent width (between 24–36 inches) in order to accommodate a wheelbarrow or mower. Also take into account the width of gateways when planning the path.

PRETTY PATHS

If the main purpose of a path is decorative, it is not necessary for it to follow the most direct route from A to B. It can dawdle and show off its charms, taking users on an exciting journey around the garden. See if you can create a path that visits all the garden's best features.

CONSULT THE PATH DOCTOR

AIM	SOLUTION 1	SOLUTION 2
I want to build the cheapest possible straight path from the house to the patio. It needs to be functional and solid.	Concrete is a good option for making a narrow path. Tamp the concrete to ensure that the path is rigid across its width.	Crushed wood chips are a cost-conscious option and can be obtained from most sawmills. When wood chips break down, they can be composted.
I want to build a pretty, winding path through a wooded area at the bottom of the garden. It has to travel from the garden up to the patio.	Stepping stones can look very natural—choose real stone slabs and set them in a bed of fine gravel. Let grass grow into the gravel.	Crushed tree bark looks good in a woodland area. Edge the path with smooth, weathered rocks or character wood such as logs and boughs.
I live by the sea and I want a path to run from the patio straight down to the water's edge. It needs to be solid and hardwearing.	Construct a pier from railroad ties. Build tracks about 6 feet apart and bridge them with the sleepers to make a long pier.	Collect large, weathered stone slabs and set them in a straight line like a set of giant stepping stones. Edge them with lengths of chain.
I want to have a decorative path running from the front door to the gate. It needs to be quietly decorative—subtle and traditional.	Red brick is a good option. Set the bricks in a herringbone pattern that is square with the sides of the path. Add a zigzag edging. (See page 40.)	A fine gravel path edged with zigzag bricks (see page 40) looks good in a formal setting. Spread the gravel over a base of hardpan.
I have just had the roof re-tiled and I would like to use the broken tiles to make a decorative path. I want to keep costs to a minimum.	Dig a trench the width of the path and lay a layer of compacted hardpan. Spread a layer of mortar and bed the tiles on edge.	Dig a trench the width of the path and edge it with brick. Tip all the broken tiles into the trench and break them into small, coin-sized pieces.
My garden is very boggy. I want a low-cost path that is dry and firm underfoot, and looks good in a natural setting.	Dig out a 12-inch-deep trench the width of the path. Half-fill it with compacted hardpan and top this with ballast followed by fine gravel.	Bang two lines of wooden piles into the ground. Link these with rails and build a wooden pier that runs clear of the ground.

Stone steps

Stone steps look beautiful, but are they hard to build?

Steps made from real or imitation stone are time-consuming to construct, involving many stages, although no one stage is particularly tricky. If you are enthusiastic, looking for a challenge, and think that you might enjoy working at a very slow, painstaking pace fitting pieces of stone together, there is no reason why you cannot build a small flight of really good-looking steps. Step-building is rather like working on an ever-changing giant jigsaw puzzle.

Steps made from salvaged flagstones. Plants have been left to seed themselves in the joints, giving a cottage garden feel.

REAL STONE

There are four readily available types of real stone: limestone, sandstone, slate, and granite. Most garden projects are best built from either natural split sandstone or reclaimed limestone.

CUTTING STONE

As far as possible, cut stone along its grain. If, like limestone, it doesn't have a pronounced grain, use an angle grinder with a stonemason's hammer and chisel. (See pages 29 and 71.)

USING MORTAR

A good, smooth mortar can be made from 2 parts cement, 1 part lime and 9 parts soft sand. (See page 13.)

FOOTINGS

An average footing is 12 inches deep, with 6 inches of compacted hardpan and 6 inches of concrete. On soft ground, make it deeper with thicker concrete. (See page 16.)

OPTIONS FOR STONE STEPS

Partially cut-in rustic steps in cleft-stone paving

↘ A long flight of cleft-stone paving steps built up a natural slope. The steps appear to be fully cut into the slope, but in fact are partially freestanding. The sides are partly visible and banked up with large rocks, so that there is a rockery to each side. This is a good project for ground that is firm and stable.

Cut-in steps in cut stone

↘ A short flight of steps cut into the side of a terrace, with the sides of the steps built into the raised walls. This is a relatively easy project, in that the earth to the back and sides, and the walls to the sides, provide support. The front and side walls are built first, leaving a gap for the steps, and the steps are then built to fit. Slabs of York stone have been used for this project.

Freestanding steps in cut stone

↘ A beautiful flight of freestanding steps running from a courtyard up to a raised patio. The steps are relatively easy to achieve in that they are built as a solid stepped block. Rough-cut field stone is used for the sides and risers, and stone slabs for the treads. Note the attractive arch feature under the steps.

HOW TO BUILD SIMPLE STEPS

These freestanding steps provide an easy option for a natural slope, or for a low flight of three or four steps. They are made from a mixture of thin pieces of split real stone for the risers, and 18-inch-square concrete pavers or slabs for the treads.

Dig out the footing trench for the first step, making it 22 inches long, 22 inches wide and 12 inches deep. Fill it with 6 inches of compacted hardpan and top with 6 inches of concrete. Once the concrete has hardened, use the split stone to build a four-walled box measuring 17 inches from front to back, and 16 inches across, to a height of about 4 inches. Fill the cavity within the box with a mixture of waste stone and concrete. Top it with mortar and bed the slabs for the treads in position.

To build the next step, repeat the procedure already described, only this time, have the top of the footing slab level with the top of the first step.

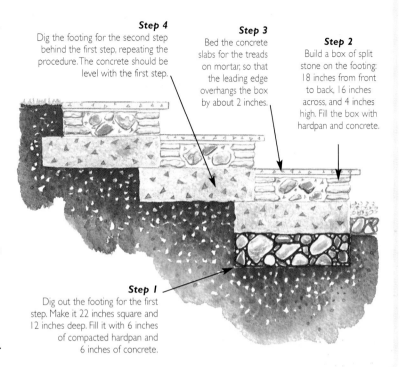

Step 4
Dig the footing for the second step behind the first step, repeating the procedure. The concrete should be level with the first step.

Step 3
Bed the concrete slabs for the treads on mortar, so that the leading edge overhangs the box by about 2 inches.

Step 2
Build a box of split stone on the footing: 18 inches from front to back, 16 inches across, and 4 inches high. Fill the box with hardpan and concrete.

Step 1
Dig out the footing for the first step. Make it 22 inches square and 12 inches deep. Fill it with 6 inches of compacted hardpan and 6 inches of concrete.

CLEFT-STONE STEPS

↘ These cleft-stone steps are built in much the same way as the simple steps described above—the difference is the way the stone for the cleft-stone treads is fitted. The secret of success is to spend a lot of time selecting the stone so that the corners of the steps are at right angles, and the leading edges at the front and sides of the treads (the nosings) are straight.

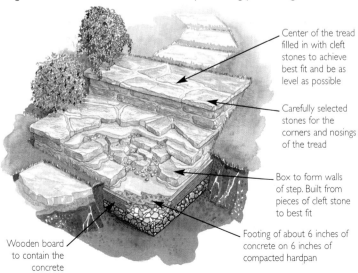

Center of the tread filled in with cleft stones to achieve best fit and be as level as possible

Carefully selected stones for the corners and nosings of the tread

Box to form walls of step. Built from pieces of cleft stone to best fit

Footing of about 6 inches of concrete on 6 inches of compacted hardpan

Wooden board to contain the concrete

MORE STONEWORK STEP DESIGNS

Much of the secret of building attractive stone steps concerns the type of stone selected for the risers. Mostly, there are two choices—you can use a stack of thin pieces of stone to make up the height of the riser, or you can use blocks that are about riser height.

It is possible to buy damaged stone from an architectural reclamation yard. Risers could be made from old limestone windowsills and suchlike, or thin pieces of old roof stone.

TROUBLESHOOTING

• Avoid using blocks of stone that need to be cut—it is much easier to use thin layers of stone.
• If the ground is unstable, dig much deeper footings and use a greater thickness of concrete.
• Stay away from the footings of the house and from drains.
• Always go for low risers rather than high ones—they are easier to build and safer to use.
• Avoid hard-to-cut stone such as granite.

Brick steps

Is brickwork as difficult as it looks?

If you can mix mortar and concrete, lift the weight of a brick, and lay one brick on top of another, you are capable of doing brickwork. Of course, to be successful you do have to make sure that each brick is vertically and horizontally level and square, and this requires patience, but brickwork is altogether much easier than it looks. It does not matter if your bricklaying is slightly less than perfect to start with—you will soon get better with practice.

TYPES OF BRICK

There are many types of brick; for garden projects, it is best to use well-fired (or high-fired) house bricks, or engineering bricks. These are harder than standard bricks, waterproof and frostproof. Low-fired interior-grade bricks are not suitable.

DESIGNING BRICK STEPS

In order to produce good brickwork, the challenge is to create a design that is mostly comprised of whole bricks (minimizing the need to cut bricks), in which the horizontal courses or layers are well bonded or interlocked, and the bricks are arranged so that the vertical joints in neighboring courses are staggered.

FOOTINGS

The bottom step in a flight always needs a solid footing of 6 inches of concrete on 6 inches of compacted hardpan. Subsequent steps only need hardpan, equal in depth to the height of the riser.

CUTTING BRICK

Usually, bricks are cut in half along their length to produce two half-bricks; sometimes, however, they are halved along their width. To cut a brick, mark a guideline with chalk, position the brick on the lawn or a piece of old carpet, set a brick chisel on the guideline, and give it a single blow with a stonemason's hammer.

USING MORTAR

Mortar should be smooth, without being too wet. When working with mortar, use a large builder's trowel to scoop it up, set it down, and to slice off the excess mortar; use a small pointing trowel to fill joints and rake out mortar to expose the edges of the bricks.

LAYING BRICKS AND KEEPING THEM LEVEL, STRAIGHT AND EVENLY SPACED

Set the brick on a bed of mortar, tapping it into place with the handle of the trowel, then butter the end with mortar. Repeat with the next brick. Every other brick or so, take a reading with the carpenter's level and make adjustments so that the bricks are aligned with each other and are both vertically and horizontally level. For beginners, it is good practice to use a carpenter's level to test each brick as it is being laid. Some beginners prefer to do the tapping process with a rubber hammer.

A beautiful flight of traditional cut-in brick steps leading from a courtyard up to a raised patio. Note the way the bricks are arranged on the leading edge of the treads so that each step curves out in a gentle convex arc.

A single step from a path to a patio, with the edge of the patio becoming the step. Note how the bricks are set upright to make a soldier course.

OPTIONS FOR BRICK STEPS

  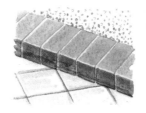 

↗ *A very basic, easy-to-build flight of steps running from a sunken patio up to a lawn.*

↗ *A flight of curved steps that reflects the shape of the large, circular brick and sett patio.*

↗ *A simple brick step, linking two nonbrick patio areas, provides an eye-catching detail.*

↗ *A basic flight of steps. The bottom step is flush with the surface of the patio.*

HOW TO BUILD BASIC BRICKWORK STEPS

Steps for soft ground
with soldier bricks forming the tread

→ This classic two-step flight of brickwork steps, with concrete over hardpan under every tread, is a good option for soft ground. The slab of concrete under every step compensates for damp clay soil.

In the project illustrated, the steps link two patios, one of which is raised slightly above the other. In this instance, there are actually three steps, with the bottom step being inset and flush with the surface of the lower patio. If you have a damp site and you want to make absolutely sure that your steps are going to stay put, with little or no movement, this is a good design to go for.

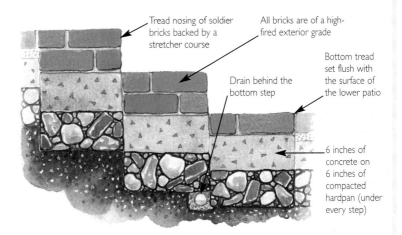

Tread nosing of soldier bricks backed by a stretcher course

All bricks are of a high-fired exterior grade

Drain behind the bottom step

Bottom tread set flush with the surface of the lower patio

6 inches of concrete on 6 inches of compacted hardpan (under every step)

Steps for a courtyard corner
with nonslip treads

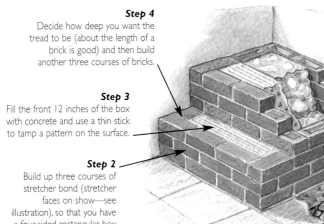

Step 4
Decide how deep you want the tread to be (about the length of a brick is good) and then build another three courses of bricks.

Step 3
Fill the front 12 inches of the box with concrete and use a thin stick to tamp a pattern on the surface.

Step 2
Build up three courses of stretcher bond (stretcher faces on show—see illustration), so that you have a four-sided rectangular box that runs back to the wall.

↙ These steps are designed to run from the corner of a courtyard to a raised patio area, and are supported at the back and on one side.

Step 5
Continue building the other steps, with the top surface of each step tamped with a pattern to make a non-slip surface.

Step 1
Dig out the whole step area to a depth of 12 inches and lay 6 inches of compacted hardpan. Top with 6 inches of concrete.

Wooden steps

I enjoy working in wood: how do I make steps?

Wooden steps are great, both for a country cottage garden or a small city patch. The level of skill required to make them depends upon the design: step construction does not have to involve complicated woodwork. For example, railroad-tie steps are heavy work, but technically they are very easy to do. The steps to raised decking (shown below center) are very straightforward because they use screws, nuts, and bolts, rather than complex joints.

This flight of steps uses full-length sleepers for the treads, quarter-sleepers for the stub (support) posts, and an infill of crushed stone.

A flight of steps running up to an area of raised decking—a simple construction with all joints either bolted or screwed.

This long flight of steps consists of pressure-treated logs for the treads, with an infill of crushed stone.

STEPS FOR RAISED DECKING

➔ The secret of these steps—the factor that makes them easy—is that all the joints are achieved by sawing standard sections of wood to length, setting one piece of wood against another, and fixing them with a couple of screws or a nut, washer, and bolt.

Banister rail

Stair treads screwed to step bearers

Support bolted to the post to hold the stringer (side joist)

Post set in a hole with hardpan and concrete

Vertical balusters screwed to rails

Step bearers screwed to a stringer (side joist)

MORE WOODEN STEPS

For the most part, the easiest way to build a flight of wooden steps—with up to four treads—is to use lengths of railroad ties. Ties are about 6 inches thick and 10 inches wide and make ideal steps, the thickness forming the riser height.

Some suppliers are happy to cut ties to suit. The most economical option is to design steps that use ties without creating any waste: for example, a 10-foot-long tie can be divided to make three 3-foot-4-inch-long steps.

Quick wooden steps

See page 45 for the quickest ways to make a flight of steps.

Natural steps

The aim of a set of natural steps is to create something that looks as if it has evolved naturally as part of the landscape—like a group of stones that makes a platform to a higher level, or fallen logs stretched across a gentle slope, behind which debris has accumulated to provide a natural step. It could be a tangle of roots that provides a foothold, or soil erosion on a slope that has formed a convenient place to move up from.

What are natural steps?

This flight of steps was designed to blend into the rockery and become a part of it. Plants assist by tumbling over the borders.

STEPS THAT BLEND IN

To blend in with nature, the steps must be made from materials such as wood or stone, and be put together in such a way that they fool you into believing that they are natural—like slabs of stone stacked on top of each other, or crushed tree bark piled behind a log, or terraces of shingle or crushed rock. Try to harmonize with the site and pick materials appropriate to the natural appearance of the area or the theme you are creating—use wood for a forest-type area, boulders and stone for a hillside, washed stone for a coast, or salvaged material for a "back to nature" inner-city site.

OPTIONS

Steps made from tree bark and logs look good in a forest-type garden, while a scree of crushed stone looks great in a hillside garden. If you live in an area that has an industrial past, you may like to consider a look that suggests that nature is taking over, by incorporating rusty iron and wooden beams.

HOW TO BUILD ROCKERY STEPS

The ideal would be to use massive weathered stones for each step, but such stones are usually too expensive to buy and too heavy to lift. An easier option is to make each step from two or three slabs of stone mortared together.

→ Set out the shape of the first step and dig a 12-inch-deep hole for the footing. Fill it with 6 inches of compacted hardpan topped with 6 inches of concrete. Take the first stone slab and bed it in mortar. Mortar the second stone on top of the first. When the first step is finished, dig away the ground behind it and pack it with hardpan as the footing for the next step. Continue as previously described.

Smaller rocks in and around the arrangement

Two smaller slabs bedded in mortar to make the second step

Hardpan packed behind the first step

12-inch-deep hole; 6 inches of concrete on 6 inches of compacted hardpan

Three large slabs mortared together to look like a weathered stone

Decorative steps

What options are there for decorative steps?

There are hundreds of ways to create steps that are a little out of the ordinary. Steps can be decorative in the sense that they have a sculpted form or shape, with curved treads or ornate rails; they can have color applied to the surface with paint or mosaics; they can be enhanced with applied carved reliefs, such as Victorian terra-cotta tiles; or the materials themselves can contribute an exciting decorative effect in stone, metal, wood, or brick.

OPTIONS FOR DECORATIVE STEPS

Although the choice is huge, you do have to choose something to fit in with your home and garden. For example, terra-cotta tiles look good in a traditional country cottage garden, decorative woodwork goes nicely with decking, mosaics of broken tiles or crockery, applied to flat surfaces, can look wonderful in a small courtyard setting, and so on. Look at your garden and home, and consider your skills and how much time you want to spend. It is best to avoid fashion statements that are likely to date.

Brick and flagstone curves

↗ *A stepped edge to a raised patio, with brick risers and flagstone treads.*

Blue decking

↗ *Wooden steps, leading up to a forest patio, are given a blue-gray colorwash for an aged effect.*

Red brick and cleft-stone paving

↗ *A traditional mix: brick for the tread nosings and cleft-stone paving for the infill.*

Blue and white

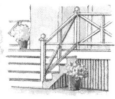

↗ *White steps with blue treads, cross-braced rails and turned post finials.*

Diamond lattice trellis

↗ *Steps leading up to a raised island patio, with lattice trellis at the sides.*

Fretted and painted pink

↗ *Decking steps with fretted and pierced details, painted a delicate pink to match the cottage.*

Country cottage green

↗ *A relaxed look—trellis with green-painted risers.*

STYLE NOTES

When you build steps, they will be as much an expression of your taste as any other feature in your house or garden, so the design deserves careful consideration. But remember that unlike rooms in your home that can be restyled fairly easily to suit changing fashions, it is more difficult to rebuild steps and so the most successful garden styles tend to be traditional, classic, and timeless.

PRACTICALITIES

As with any steps, it is most important that decorative steps are safe. However you choose to adorn them, the decoration must not pose a hazard.

So if, for example, you were thinking about decorating the steps with glazed tiles or shells, they should be kept to the sides and the risers, and not applied to the treads, because these must have a level, nonslip surface. Always make safety a priority.

Building tips

The decoration has to survive extremes of weather—sun, wind, and rain.

Brick ~ Use high-fired water- and frost-resistant bricks. (See page 58.)

Stone ~ Lay stone with the run of the grain on one of the edge faces, rather than uppermost, so that it doesn't collect water. (See page 56.)

Paint and finishes ~ Use paints, varnishes, and finishes that are designed for outdoor use.

Ceramic tiles ~ Use high-fired quarry tiles for large areas. If you want to incorporate areas of mosaic made of broken bathroom tiles or crockery, use waterproof cement and grout.

Doorsteps

A doorstep undoubtedly needs to be fit for its purpose—to get you from one level to another—but its secondary function (some would say most important function) is to form a visual introduction to the house. The doorstep (consisting of one or more steps) needs to be attractive and welcoming, and can also convey more subtle messages—for example, the design might declare that you have good taste, or the large size hint that you are generous.

What makes a perfect doorstep?

DOORSTEP OPTIONS

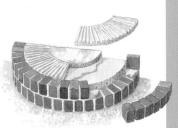

↗ *A single step with a porch over it and seats to the side makes a grand entrance.*

↗ *Two flights of cleft-stone steps leading up a gentle slope, with a short linking path.*

↗ *A generous pair of decking steps built over a single existing high brick step.*

↗ *A semicircular step built from half-bricks and half of a patio circle tile-and-slab kit.*

STYLE

Doorsteps are quite a challenge: they must get you comfortably from one level to another, look sufficiently grand and welcoming, and they also have to draw your eye up to the door. It is best to choose a design with a low riser height—no more than 6 inches—and the broadest possible width.

IMPORTANT NOTES

Doorsteps have three important elements—riser height, tread depth and step width. You need to get them all right.

Riser height ~ A good, comfortable, easy-to-use doorstep has risers that are no lower than 4 inches and no higher than 6 inches, with all the risers in the flight of steps the same height.

Tread depth ~ The tread depth (the distance from the tread nosing, or edge, back to the face of the next riser) must be made up from one or more foot-lengths—no shorter than 9 inches and as long as you like.

Step width ~ The step needs to be at least as wide as the doorway—say, about 28 inches—but the wider the better. One good option is to have the steps fanning out from the doorway in a series of ever-widening curves.

HOW TO BUILD A BRICK DOORSTEP

⬂ This traditional doorstep is made from old, high-fired bricks. The riser height is equal to half a brick (about 4½ inches). Lay a 6-inch-thick concrete footing slab for the bottom step. Set the bottom row of soldier bricks in place to make the first riser, half-fill the resultant cavity with concrete, and lay the bricks that make the bottom tread. Build the second riser, and continue up the flight. When you get to paving the top step, the bricks are laid in a stretcher bond for the straight bit, and a herringbone for the quarter-circle.

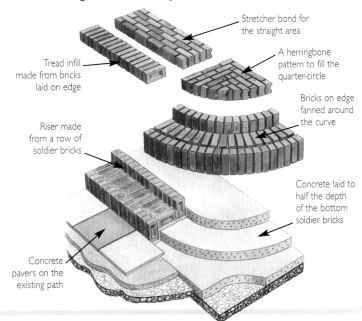

Stretcher bond for the straight area

A herringbone pattern to fill the quarter-circle

Bricks on edge fanned around the curve

Tread infill made from bricks laid on edge

Riser made from a row of soldier bricks

Concrete laid to half the depth of the bottom soldier bricks

Concrete pavers on the existing path

Patio furniture

Could I use a few old chairs from the house?

Patio furniture needs to be attractive, inviting, well built, designed for the job, and above all comfortable. Furnish your patio with the same care as a room in your home. Don't rush into making a purchase—instead, wait until you are sure of your requirements and then shop around.

A combined bench and table is especially useful if you plan to eat out in the garden with the children.

SUITABILITY

Think about how you plan to use the patio, and decide what type of furniture you need to fulfil these needs. Are you just going to sit on the patio for the occasional half hour to read a newspaper, in which case a bench or chairs would be suitable, or do you intend to sunbathe, in which case a lounger would be more appropriate? If you would like to eat outdoors, do you need a small occasional table for snacks, a larger, family-size combined bench and table, or something more elegant for entertaining?

➔ *A "steamer" chair is both attractive and comfortable, offering the opportunity to lounge in style.*

↗ *This easy-to-move wheeled bench has an integral table, making it doubly useful.*

Requirements		Options
Dining *We want a table big enough for the family. It must be strong, with an easy-wipe surface so that I don't have to worry about spills. It must suit a country garden.*		There are lots of options, such as plastic tables with separate chairs, or metal dining suites, but the best option for a family is a wooden table. Spills do not matter—you just scrub it down with soap and water.
Reclining *I want a really comfortable recliner. It must be strong, but light enough for me to move on my own. It has got to be modern and appropriate for a design-conscious city garden.*		Wooden recliners look good, and metal recliners are relatively inexpensive, but you cannot do better than some of the large plastic recliners—they are light, attractive, and amazingly comfortable.
Style is important *We are seeking some really stylish furniture, because we do a lot of entertaining and need to impress clients. We have a large garden with lots of designer features. Money no object.*		If you want something extra-special, and are not worried about the cost, you could contact an architect or designer who specializes in one-off designs, and maybe have something built in marble or stainless steel.
Mostly ornamental *We want furniture to blend in with our traditional Victorian house. We like lots of ornamental details and want to leave the furniture out in the garden as a permanent feature.*		The best solution is to buy some genuine or reproduction Victorian cast-iron furniture. Some architectural reclamation yards specialize in Victorian pieces. Avoid anything that looks cracked.
Stacking, folding or knock-down *We are looking for furniture for our very small town garden. We will need to put it away for the winter, in a small shed and a loft space over the garage, so it must be lightweight.*		There are many easy-to-store options, but they often compromise on comfort. One traditional fold-up design, back in fashion, is the deckchair with canvas seat. It is both comfortable and easy to store.

MATERIALS AND STYLES

Victorian reproduction

Patio furniture comes in a huge choice of materials and styles—wood, metal, plastic, modern, traditional, high-tech, and so on. When deciding what to buy, take into account the style of your garden. A modern, minimalist city yard might be best served by contemporary metalwork or plastic, or design classics. More traditional country and cottage-style gardens would welcome wooden furniture—choose from classic hardwood designs, rustic concoctions, or folk-style shapes. Stonework also blends well into traditional gardens, and can be used to create permanent, weatherproof benches. These look striking, but are not the most comfortable option to choose.

← *Reproduction Victorian cast-iron furniture, made of aluminum, looks stylish and is much lighter than the original.*

Folding, rigid, and reclining

↗ *Three chair options. A slanted back is more comfortable than an upright one.*

Rustic

↗ *Rustic furniture looks good in a country garden. You will need cushions for comfort.*

Classical

↗ *Stone is good if you value classic longevity over comfort.*

↗ *A wooden "steamer" recliner harmonizes perfectly with a decking patio.*

Design classic

↗ *Look for designer chairs at yard sales.*

Teak

↗ *Teak is long-lasting. Buy it from a reputable sustainable source.*

Folk

↗ *Folk-style chairs can be made cheaply from salvaged wood.*

QUICK AND EASY FURNITURE SOLUTIONS

Instant furniture can be made from planks and concrete blocks: just stack the blocks and lay planks across them to make tables and benches. Seats from classic cars make inexpensive, comfortable, arty furniture. Traditional seaside deckchairs are reasonably cheap, and are available in strong colors and patterns that will jazz up any patio.

THINGS TO AVOID

Avoid furniture that relies on springs and elastic, because it is not durable. Stainless-steel patio furniture may have weak bolts, and if one of these shears off, it renders the item useless. Make sure you only buy items that are weatherproof and can be safely left outside, unless you are prepared to dash out when rain threatens and bring them indoors.

Safety

Fold-up chairs are a bad idea if children and older people will be using them, especially if the clips and locks are fragile. Such chairs have a nasty habit of folding up and nipping fingers.

Some plastics eventually become brittle and make chairs liable to collapse if you lean back on them.

WINTER STORAGE

Apart from furniture that is built in situ, or made from heavy oak, most pieces need to be stored for the winter. Even plastic quickly degrades when it is left out in all weathers. Think about where you are going to put it before purchasing.

MAINTENANCE

At the end of the season, wooden furniture needs to be protected with paint, teak oil, or creosote. Traditionally, gardeners used to brush large benches and chairs with creosote and set them upside down in a shed. Modern plastic and metal chairs are best wiped over with a damp cloth and stored in a dry place. Soft cushions should be stored in plastic bags and kept inside the house, in dry and warm conditions, away from possible colonization by mice. Use a small paintbrush to dab springs and bolts with a light oil, to stop rust.

Furniture you can make

Is it hard to make some furniture for the patio?

There is a long tradition of householders making garden furniture (such as porch chairs, swings, picnic benches and, of course, patio furniture) from whatever was at hand. In the United States, old crates were used to make Adirondack chairs, in Germany and Switzerland furniture was constructed from rough-sawn lumber, and in England rustic chairs were fashioned from fruit tree wood. Enthusiasm is more important than technical ability: there is a project for everyone.

IS IT WORTH MAKING MY OWN GARDEN FURNITURE?

Making your own garden furniture is very worthwhile—it can be done for almost no cost, the results are long-lasting and stylish, and the whole activity is very enjoyable. There is nothing quite so satisfying as sitting in a chair you have made and listening to friends admire your handiwork. There are projects suitable for all abilities—you can try anything from a very basic, straightforward piece such as a built-in bench, to something more involved, such as an Adirondack chair. All can be made using a minimum of tools and equipment.

← A classic example of an Adirondack chair, made from old crates fixed with screws. This one is special, in that it folds up for storage.

INSPIRATIONS

Visit a museum and look at farmhouse and folk furniture of the past (such as three-legged stools, board tables, and plank-back chairs) to get inspiration, and then have a go. Limit yourself to using simple hand tools and basic hammer and nail joints.

THE POSSIBILITIES

PERMANENT (BUILT-IN) FURNITURE

- Tables and benches can be made from stacks of concrete blocks topped with heavy planks or railroad ties.
- Chairs and benches can be built entirely from bricks.
- A bench can be made from two sections cut from a sturdy pole (these make the two supports) bridged with a plank.
- Low walls always attract people to sit on them—consider building special walls of just the right height.

MOVABLE FURNITURE

- Chairs and benches can be made from willow wands nailed together. Start with a simple stool form—a plank seat and four legs—and then try adding arms and a backrest.
- A low stool can be made from a section cut from a tree. If you want to move it, you tip it over and roll it.
- A heavy bench can be maneuvered with ease if you give it a pair of wheels and a handle, rather like a long wheelbarrow.
- A traditional wooden picnic table is light enough to move easily. If you want to follow the sun or shade, you simply lift or drag it to a new location.

WOOD

- Railroad ties make good benches. Make sure you avoid those that are oozing oil and tar.
- The wood from old fruit trees is good for making rustic furniture—the wood is scented and an exciting shape.
- Thin willow wands can be woven into screens or chair backs.
- Wood that has been pressure-treated with preservative is not suitable for tabletops that will hold food, unless varnished.

STONE

- Benches can be built using cut stone topped with planks.
- Small stone cairns (small pillars built with field stone and mortar) make good stools and table legs.

METAL

- Tables, chairs and benches can be built using exhibition-grade aluminum scaffolding, with scaffolding clips for joints.
- Old tractor seats make attractive and stylish stools.

Important dimensions

There are certain standard dimensions for furniture (measure manufactured pieces in your home), but you might have to make changes to suit your needs. For example, a standard upright chair is 16³/₄ inches high, but if you are above or below average height, or are making an easy chair, you will have to make adjustments.

Make a mock-up

To test out dimensions, make a mock-up—use a box for a chair, and a pile of bricks for a table. Make a series of gradual adjustments to the mock-up until it feels correct and comfortable.

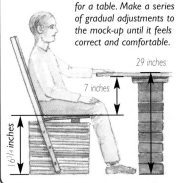

29 inches

7 inches

16³/₄ inches

HOW TO BUILD A STONE TABLE

The pillar is made of thin, random pieces of stone such as reclaimed roof stone (split limestone) or field stone, and three slabs about 3 inches thick. The base slab and capital slab can be any type of flagstone; for the tabletop you may prefer to use a slate or limestone flagstone, which has more character.

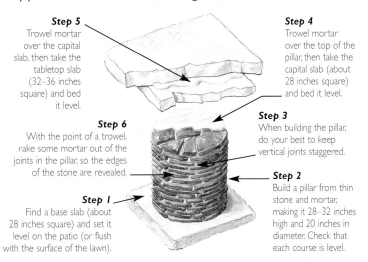

Step 5
Trowel mortar over the capital slab, then take the tabletop slab (32–36 inches square) and bed it level.

Step 4
Trowel mortar over the top of the pillar, then take the capital slab (about 28 inches square) and bed it level.

Step 6
With the point of a trowel, rake some mortar out of the joints in the pillar, so the edges of the stone are revealed.

Step 3
When building the pillar, do your best to keep vertical joints staggered.

Step 1
Find a base slab (about 28 inches square) and set it level on the patio (or flush with the surface of the lawn).

Step 2
Build a pillar from thin stone and mortar, making it 28–32 inches high and 20 inches in diameter. Check that each course is level.

HOW TO MAKE WOODEN SEATING

This corner bench is made from standard sections of rough-sawn wood directly from the sawmill. The seat is supported by four side leg frames, and one corner leg frame, each consisting of two legs joined at the top by a stretcher or linking bar (two for the corner frame). Seat boards are fixed to the leg frames, and the front edges of the seat are finished with fascia strips. The whole structure is fixed with two lag screws at each joint, and finished with water-based, exterior-grade paint. The attractive herringbone miter joint where the two halves of the bench meet is created by butting the seat boards end to side, and then side to end, with each successive strip.

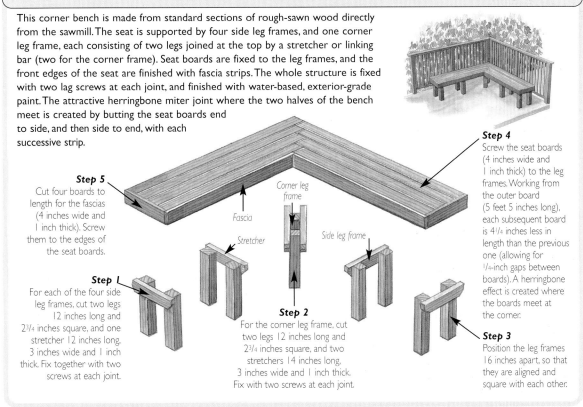

Step 5
Cut four boards to length for the fascias (4 inches wide and 1 inch thick). Screw them to the edges of the seat boards.

Step 1
For each of the four side leg frames, cut two legs 12 inches long and 2³/₄ inches square, and one stretcher 12 inches long, 3 inches wide and 1 inch thick. Fix together with two screws at each joint.

Corner leg frame

Fascia

Stretcher

Side leg frame

Step 2
For the corner leg frame, cut two legs 12 inches long and 2³/₄ inches square, and two stretchers 14 inches long, 3 inches wide and 1 inch thick. Fix with two screws at each joint.

Step 4
Screw the seat boards (4 inches wide and 1 inch thick) to the leg frames. Working from the outer board (5 feet 5 inches long), each subsequent board is 4¹/₄ inches less in length than the previous one (allowing for ¹/₄-inch gaps between boards). A herringbone effect is created where the boards meet at the corner.

Step 3
Position the leg frames 16 inches apart, so that they are aligned and square with each other.

Planting for patios

What is the best way to fill a patio with plants?

Patios are usually designed to be sheltered and warm, and are often a contrasting environment to the rest of the garden. There are three key things to remember when selecting plants for patio containers: choose varieties suitable for a container in the allocated position, whether sunny or shady, water regularly, and feed periodically according to the plant's requirements. Pots, troughs, raised beds, and hanging baskets can all play a part.

Planting options

Containers ~ A container can be anything from a ceramic pot to an old watering can. Just add a drainage hole at the bottom if there isn't one.

Planters ~ Planters are larger and heavier versions of containers—for example, a lead tank or an old sink.

Trellis or arbor ~ Good for supporting climbing plants and can also be used as a screen. (See page 70.)

Planting pockets ~ You can leave slabs or bricks out of the patio surface to make pockets for small plants.

An old stone sink propped up on bricks, and a large ceramic pot, make perfect partners on a traditional brick patio.

HOW TO GET STARTED

Study your patio and then make a list to describe the conditions (such as dry or shady), the role you want the plants to play, and the way you wish to display the plants.

For example, let's say that your patio is very sunny, you want to have climbing plants all around to give shade and privacy, and you want the plants to be displayed in large ceramic pots. The climbers will have to be mainly evergreen to provide a screen, and tolerant of sun and dry conditions. Certain varieties of clematis, jasmine, and honeysuckle might be suitable.

CONTAINER OPTIONS

If we define a container as being smaller than a planter—so it can be moved with relative ease—it can consist of anything from a large can to a chimney pot. There are many exciting options. You could make a collection of galvanized buckets, watering cans, or old cooking pots. Anything that is free from sharp edges, and large enough to house your patio plants, is suitable. A group of ceramic pots, in the same color, will make a visual impact and provide the patio with a consistent theme.

An old galvanized bucket is an attractive container for small plants.

Pots are an easy option and good when you want to group plants.

Hanging baskets look good cascading from an arbor over the patio.

Unattractive plastic pots can be disguised in an outer container like an old galvanized bathtub.

Old-fashioned chimney pots make striking display stands, perfect for a special planting feature.

PLANTER OPTIONS

Planters are much the same as containers, only bigger—once they are in place and bulging with plants, they are pretty much immovable. The point here is that unlike containers that can easily be moved to suit your whims, a planter is usually installed and then left alone. In other words, planters require a lot of forward planning—the shape, the size, the position, and, of course, the way the plants within the planter are going to be selected and grouped—so that you do not make mistakes.

A dwarf evergreen in a picket box.

A long picket trough concealing plastic pots—useful if you want an ever-changing display.

A wooden trough with an integral trellis.

A planter made from a reconstituted stone kit. The blocks all fit together like a puzzle and are bonded with mortar or resin.

A stone sink mounted on a length of sleeper.

HOW TO MAKE A STONE RAISED BED

PLANTING POCKETS

Permanent raised beds are a great option for an existing stone or brick patio. They can be built using easily obtainable materials such as bricks or concrete blocks, positioned precisely where you want them and, best of all, built to a height and size to suit your specific needs. The only proviso is that the patio must be well built, with a strong footing of compacted hardpan. For ease, design a rectilinear or square bed (so that it can be made from whole bricks as much as possible) to fit within the grid of your patio.

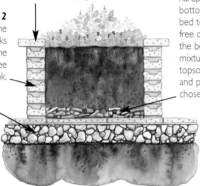

Step 3
Build the walls with bricks and mortar, staggering the joints in the courses. Rake mortar out of a vertical joint at the bottom of the bed for drainage. Spread a generous layer of mortar on the top course; bed the coping slabs in place.

Step 4
Put loose hardpan in the bottom of the bed to promote free drainage. Fill the bed with a mixture of topsoil and peat, and plant your chosen plants.

Step 2
Design the bed so that the sides are built of whole bricks as much as possible. Lay the courses of bricks (dry) to see how the bed will look.

Step 1
Make sure that the patio is well built, with a footing of concrete or compacted hardpan. If you are not sure, lift the paving to check.

A few bricks have been omitted from this patio to provide a planting pocket that has been filled with low, creeping plants.

This delightful feature, incorporated into a stone wall, is the perfect home for a slow-growing, drooping variety.

Container and tub planting guide

A patio is the perfect place for feature containers, planters, and raised beds. Perhaps you need climbing plants to tumble and cascade from an overhead arbor, or you want to be surrounded by whispering grasses. Maybe you like the idea of sitting amid a jungle of old-fashioned cottage garden plants. The listings below will give you a few ideas to get you started.

Favorite flowers	Good foliage	Just bulbs	Good combinations
Snapdragon *Antirrhinum majus* A short-lived perennial providing lots of color. Dwarf varieties look good in grouped containers. Prefers full sun.	**Plantain lily** *Hosta* "Ginko Craig" Leaves with white margins and lots of compact, bell-shaped flowers.	**Golden garlic** *Allium moly* Bright yellow flowers. Likes a rocky soil and lots of sun.	**Bright summer color** Flame creeper and Chinese Virginia creeper *Tropaeoleum speciosum; Parthenocissus henryana* Flame creeper has bright red flowers; Chinese Virginia creeper has green or bronze leaves. An exotic mix of climbers, perfect for an arbor.
Pimpernel *Anagallis monellii* Beautiful blue flowers with pink centers. A dwarf bushy tender perennial, which flowers from summer until the fall.	**Red-hot poker** *Kniphofia* "Little Maid" Grass-like leaves and pale yellow flowers.	**Daffodil** *Narcissus* Many shades available; looks good in clumps.	**Cottage plants** Pansy and stonecrop *Viola* "Molly Sanderson"; *Sedum kamtschaticum* The intense purple flowers of the pansies and the golden-orange flowers of the stonecrop make a stunning combination for a low border.
European daisy *Bellis perennis* A mass of very pretty pom-pon flowers in red, pink, or white. Likes sun or partial shade.	**Dead nettle** *Lamium maculatum* Nettle-like leaves; various leaf colors.	**Windflower** *Anemone blanda* Blue flowers. Likes sun and well-drained soil.	**Climbers** Honeysuckle and climbing snapdragon *Lonicera periclymenum; Asarina antirrhinifolia* The exotic flowers of the honeysuckle look great with the violet flowers of the snapdragon.
	Cobweb houseleek *Sempervivum arachnoideum* Decorative leaf rosettes.	**Indian shot plant** *Canna* hybrids Tall, exotic, and showy. Needs sun.	
Patience plant *Impatiens* cultivars Lots of red, pink, white, or orange flowers. Likes a rich soil. Thrives in sun or partial shade.	**Creeping Jenny** *Lysimachia nummularia* "Aurea" Striking golden leaves.	**Snake's head fritillary** *Fritillaria meleagris* White, purple, and pink flowers in spring.	**Just grasses** Blue fescue and Chinese fountain grass *Festuca glauca; Pennisetum alopecuroides* Blue fescue looks stunning alongside the tall rust-brown plumes of the fountain grass.

Arbors and trellises

Are attractive arbors and trellises hard to build?

A trellis is not a very sophisticated object—just a number of thin, rough-sawn battens fixed together with nails—but when it is in place and covered with climbing plants, it can totally transform a patio. Much the same goes for an arbor, which is just a collection of beams, and yet can become a real feature. Arbors are easy to build, because the construction is just basic woodwork. Trellises are readily available at garden centers, but also simple to make yourself.

ARBORS

An arbor can turn a patio into an exciting living area, which is more of a sophisticated room than a paved area. It makes the patio feel more defined and solid. Once an arbor is draped in plants, it becomes a beautiful, shady retreat—a true green room.

Arbor options

A corner arbor with integral screen and seat

An open arbor— just a plant support

A roof designed to give maximum shade

A porch-type arbor with lattice screens

A simple design made with rustic poles

A design to match the style of the house

How to make an arbor

An arbor is made up from four elements: main posts, beams that link the posts, rafters that sit on the beams, and battens that top the lot.

A simple arbor structure

Step 3
Bridge the beams with rafters set at right angles

Step 4
Bridge the rafters with a roof of battens.

Step 2
Bridge the posts with beams. Fix the joints with metal straps or patent fixings.

Step 1
Set the main posts in holes 12 inches deep; top up each hole with concrete.

Beam and rafter shapes

Cyma curve

Classic round nose

Simple angle

Modern round nose

Concave curve

Quarter round

TRELLISES

At one level, a trellis is no more than a frame designed to support a climbing plant, but it can also be a highly patterned, eye-catching feature, which is more an architectural statement than a mere support for plants.

Trellis types range from a very simple, store-bought lattice of slats that you screw directly to the wall of your house, to a freestanding screen complete with an arched top, one or more doorways, and posts with carved finials. However, it is also easy to make your own trellis, using low-cost materials and the simplest of hand tools—a saw, a drill, and a hammer. If you would like to enhance your patio with a stunning decorative feature, now is your chance.

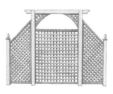

↗ *A trellis designed to be used as a backdrop for a special sculpture.*

↗ *A portable hinged and folding trellis screen.*

↗ *A folding trellis designed as a corner feature.*

Good plants for an arbor or trellis

The essence of a successful arbor or trellis is of course the plants that clothe it and embellish the wooden structure. The following plants are all climbers, which draw the eye upward.

Evergreen with feature leaves
Algerian ivy (*Hedera canariensis*): glossy leaves, red stems
Colchis (*Hedera colchica*): large, heart-shaped leaves
English ivy (*Hedera helix*): various colors, self-clinging

Perennial with feature flowers or fruit
Common hop (*Humulus lupulus* 'Aureus'): gold leaves, hop flowers
Sweet honeysuckle (*Lonicera caprifolium*): orange berries
Snail flower (*Phaseolus caracalla*): orange-yellow flowers, beans

Perennial and annual with scented flowers
Clematis—early (*Clematis montana* f. *grandiflora*): white flowers
Clematis—late (*Clematis tangutica*): yellow, bell-like flowers
Cup-and-saucer vine (*Cobaea scandens*): cream to purple flowers

Note: common names and varieties vary from region to region

Walls and dividers

Building a wall might look like a difficult job, but is in fact a series of small, easy tasks. Most brick walls are built with the stretcher or header face of the brick on view. Each row is called a course, and the wall is usually topped with a coping. The pattern bricks are laid in is termed the bond. The object of the bond is to stagger the vertical joints in order to create a strong wall. A simple stretcher bond can be used to create either a single- or double-brick wall.

I have never built a wall: is it difficult?

STONE WALLS

Stone walls are usually built up from thin, flat pieces of stone bedded in mortar. If it is necessary to cut stone, use found pieces of a type that splits down into easy-to-use, square-faced pieces. Support the stone on a piece of old carpet, and use a stonemason's hammer with a brick chisel for general cutting, or a cold chisel for more delicate cutting.

If existing brick or stone walls are in a poor condition, there are ways to brighten them up. The quickest solution is to paint the whole area. You could plant climbers (against trellis panels fixed to the walls if you wish). If you want a thorough renovation of the walls, rent a sand blaster to clean back the surface, and then make good-quality repairs.

➜ *This impressive patio water feature has been built without changing the underlying structure of the patio or the wall—no digging or construction work. The plant has transformed the wall.*

↗ *A country garden wall made from cut stone, old bricks, and tiles.*

↗ *A retaining wall with a coping top and an integral bench seat, made from reconstituted stone blocks.*

QUICK IDEAS FOR DIVIDING UP YOUR PATIO AREA

Folding screens ~ A three-part trellis screen can be opened out and repositioned to suit the changing position of the sun and the direction of the wind.

Hanging plants ~ Basket plants can be hung from an arbor to create a fast-growing screen of cascading foliage.

Drapes ~ An area can be curtained off with one of the modern pavilion tents, or best of all with a traditional striped canvas awning, providing shade and privacy.

HOW TO BUILD A WALL IN BRICK OR STONE

Brick and stone garden walls need a solid footing. As a general guide, the concrete footing slab must be two to three times the width of the proposed wall. (Err on the side of caution and make a thicker, wider slab if you are uncertain.) Dry-stone walls are made of carefully stacked stones and do not use mortar. See also pages 32–33, 48–49, 58–59 (brick); 26–27, 28–29, 56–57 (stone).

Safety notes

If a brick or stone garden wall is to be more than chest height, you must dig a deeper trench—say ,16 inches deep—and increase the thickness of the concrete slab to 8–10 inches.

Freestanding brick wall, one brick thick

Step 4
Use a trowel to rake out excess mortar and to tool it to an angled finish.

Step 3
Use a carpenter's level to check that every brick is vertically and horizontally level.

Step 2
Lay the courses of bricks with mortar, staggering the vertical joints.

Step 1
Dig a trench 12 inches deep and 12 inches wide. Fill with 4 inches of compacted hardpan and 4 inches of concrete.

Freestanding wall made of field stone

Step 4
Select stones with one straight face, and place them on top of the wall with this face outermost.

Step 3
Lay the stone with staggered vertical joints and long "tie" stones running through the thickness of the wall.

Step 2
Fill the trench with 4 inches of compacted hardpan followed by 8 inches of concrete.

Step 1
Dig a trench 16 inches deep and three times the width of the wall.

Ornaments and decoration

A patio is a place that you can decorate and embellish to your heart's content—it can be anything you want it to be. Treat your patio as a blank canvas, and let rip and enjoy yourself. Perhaps you are inspired by Victoriana, stark minimalism, Celtic art, American folk art, or all things gold: the possibilities for interesting decorative effects are numerous. You can even treat the area as an exhibition space, and change the display theme frequently.

Birds will love this reconstituted stone cat! Sculptures of animals are a perennial favorite for the garden.

PLANNING YOUR LOOK

The bottom line about designing a patio space complete with ornaments and decoration is that in order to realize your vision, you have to plan methodically—even if you want it to be a shrine to anarchic chaos. For example, if you want the patio to be covered with decorative mosaics, you will need to provide surfaces to create them on. If you want to display a collection of bonsai, you will need lots of small niches. A statue might be displayed to best effect by building a small plinth.

Sculpture

A traditional brick and stone patio is the perfect place to display sculpture, such as ceramic figures, ironwork, cast concrete busts or three-dimensional mosaics. Consider how you want the sculpture to be viewed and then shape the space accordingly, with blank walls and niches.

TOPIARY

If you want topiary as a patio feature, don't lose sight of the fact that it is a living plant. Not only does it need sunlight, watering, and just the right soil conditions, it will also increase in size. You must take these factors into account when including topiary in your design.

IDEAS AND GUIDELINES FOR PATIO ORNAMENTS AND DECORATION

Mosaics

Mosaics can be embedded into walls and floors, or used as surface decoration for structures such as brick-built benches and tables. Use either traditional glass tiles, ceramic tiles, or even items such as pebbles, shells, or broken crockery.

Wall features

Patio walls provide the perfect display space for weatherproof items that you have collected on your travels, such as ethnic masks or carved reliefs.

Bird bath

An attractive bird bath will entice birds and give you plenty of activity to watch as they enjoy splashing about. Place it so that you can view it from your favorite patio chair, or perhaps from a room in your house.

Pots

Pots are uniquely exciting in that they are both decorative and hold plants. Consider setting them at various levels to create a cascade of color.

Ironwork

Decorative and functional ironwork items—such as shelf brackets, candle holders, screens, old farm and garden tools, and containers—can be hung on walls. There are many possibilities for adding an unusual flourish.

Found items

Chance finds can make interesting patio features, for example a pile of unusual stones, a scattering of shells, a few fossils, or a heap of driftwood.

Sculptures

A single statue, a group of figures, or even a collection of amusing gnomes will all provide a focus of interest.

ORNAMENTS YOU CAN BUY

A patio without ornament is like an empty room—a rather sad place. However, a thoughtfully planned patio should not look cluttered—be selective when choosing ornaments, and don't be tempted to fill the patio until it is bulging with items that you don't really want or need. Start with just a few core items and proceed from there.

↗ *A patio is the perfect place for displaying sculpture. The huge choice of figurative items includes angels, classical figures, gnomes, pixies, rabbits, dogs, cats, and pigs; abstract items encompass glass, ceramic, concrete, metal spheres and cones, or stone and metal cubes.*

↗ *A small, self-contained water feature will enliven a tiny patio. You have a choice between abstract and figurative.*

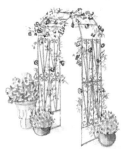

↗ *Ceramic pots often look so good that they can be regarded more as pieces of sculpture than functional containers—there is a vast choice from plain to glazed in a range of colors; there are also some huge feature pots that can host a stunning display.*

↗ *Real fossils always look good— the Victorians displayed them in their walled gardens. Today you can also buy good imitations.*

↗ *Ironwork suits patios. Balusters, furniture, brackets, plant supports, and rose arches contribute a rustic feel.*

↗ *Standing stones were once rare and expensive, but are now easy to buy. They make a perfect patio centerpiece.*

MAKE YOUR OWN ART AND SCULPTURE

A leaping fish design made from pieces of broken bathroom tile and crockery stuck on with tile cement.

Making patio art and sculptures is a wonderfully stimulating and therapeutic opportunity that should not be missed. Even if you are a novice, remember that the pleasure you derive from the process is equally as important as the finished results.

Mosaic pictures for patio walls
Mosaics are easy—just draw out the design, use a suitable waterproof adhesive or tile cement to stick down small pieces of glass tile, ceramic tile, or broken pottery to make up the design, and then fill the joints with a waterproof grout. Clean excess grout off the surface before it dries.

Slate urns and creative shapes
Old roofing slate is a great material for building abstract sculptures. Decide on the form you want to create and draw it to size. Cut a template out of card or plywood, to follow the profile of the walls of the item. Build the walls with slate and mortar to the desired shape. Keep using the template to check that the side profile is correct. When the form is nearly finished, complete by using mortar to hold the slate in place.

An urn made by building slate walls according to a template profile.

Found objects
When it comes to decorative found objects, anything goes—one man's junk is another man's patio art.

Natural ~ Found objects from nature are wonderful and uniquely beautiful— rocks, shells, driftwood, bundles of twigs, stones covered in lichen, tree bark, stones pierced with holes, fossils, bleached bones, and pieces of wood that have been shaped by wind and rain.

Man-made ~ If you like old car wheel hubs, rusty buckets, discarded farm tools, or old chimney pots, now is your chance to start a collection.

DON'T FORGET SAFETY
If you intend to display items such as farm implements, remember that they might be dangerous, especially in the hands of children. Make them harmless by fixing them beyond reach on a wall, or enclose them in some way so that inquisitive fingers are unable to explore.

Ponds

Is a patio a good place to have a pond?

Ponds are uniquely fascinating structures and can form a symbiotic relationship with a patio. A pond can be built on an existing patio or alongside it, to a sunken or raised design. It can contain a fountain, fish, or plants. A pond always excites interest, and can liven up a space that is pleasant but unremarkable.

STYLE, SHAPE AND SIZE

If you want to create a small, easy-to-build pond—geometrical or irregular—without disturbing the integrity of the patio, it is best to build a raised pond that sits on the patio. Conversely, if you want a large pond, don't mind disturbing the surface of the patio, and are prepared for lots of work digging a hole and mixing concrete, create a sunken pond flush with the ground.

Measure your patio and consider a shape, size, and style for the proposed pond. Visit a water garden center to look at examples.

Ponds have to be lined in order to hold water. The most common methods are either to use a preformed rigid liner or a sheet of flexible butyl rubber.

↗ *A partially sunken pond built from rendered concrete blocks with mosaic designs applied.*
→ *A raised pond made of brick with a coping of reconstituted stone slabs. It has a rigid liner.*

POND OPTIONS

POND LININGS

There are three methods of ensuring that a pond holds water. You can use a preformed plastic or resin liner, a flexible liner, or lay concrete.

Preformed liners ~ These rigid liners look tempting in their simplicity, but they are expensive, small, and surprisingly tricky to fit. Resin ones last longer than those made of polypropylene.

Flexible liners ~ If you want to build a pond to your own design—to any size—a flexible liner is the best choice. Top-quality butyl will last years. Two layers of synthetic padding will protect it from being pierced by stones.

Concrete lining ~ If you enjoy hard work and want a long-lasting pond at the lowest possible cost, concrete is the traditional answer.

Raised pond

↑ A very simple raised pond built into the corner of an existing patio, matching an existing brick wall. The edge of the preformed rigid liner has been covered by the top row of bricks.
↗ A small, square, formal sunken pond with a stone paver edging, built as the central feature within an existing patio. The double-thickness concrete block wall has been rendered with mortar and brushed with waterproof pond paint.

Sunken pond

Fish and plants

Fish ~ There is a choice: you can either introduce fish, or you can let native wildlife take over and wait for frogs, newts, and suchlike to appear. You cannot easily have both.

Plants ~ The primary object of planting a pond is to achieve a "balance" between the amounts of oxygen and algae in the water. This ensures clear, sweet water.

HOW TO BUILD A RAISED POND

Using a flexible liner

↘ A raised pond can be built to any shape you wish by constructing a brick cavity ring wall on a concrete slab, with a flexible butyl liner laid across the base (and then running up between the cavity walls). A thin layer of concrete is spread over the base to protect the liner.

Using a preformed liner

↘ A preformed rigid liner is put in position on a concrete slab, and a brick ring wall built around it. The lip of the liner rests on the wall. The space between the inner face of the wall and the liner is packed with sand to give additional support to the liner.

Step 5
Cut the coping tiles to fit, so that they bridge the two walls and trap the liner, and bed them on mortar.

Step 4
Where the liner exits the cavity wall, cut away the protective padding to reveal the butyl. Fold it toward the pond and trim flush with the edge of the wall.

Step 2
Lay the butyl across the footing and build the cavity wall. (The butyl is sandwiched between the two walls and the top edge is trapped under the coping tiles.)

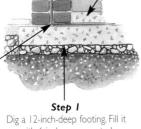

Step 3
Float 2 inches of concrete over the liner.

Step 1
Dig a 12-inch-deep footing. Fill it with 6 inches compacted hardpan and 6 inches concrete.

Step 4
Spread mortar on top of the walls and bed the coping tiles in place.

Step 3
Position the liner on the slab and build a double-thickness brick wall around it, filling the cavity between the liner and the wall with sand as you go.

Step 2
Dig the footing to a depth of 12 inches, then fill it with 6 inches of compacted hardpan and cover with 6 inches of concrete. (The central area will contain sand to support the liner.)

Step 1
Calculate the size of the footing and mark it on the ground with pegs and string.

HOW TO BUILD A SUNKEN POND

Carefully cut reconstituted stone slabs to fit around your chosen pond diameter. Dig the hole and spread a sandwich of padding, butyl rubber, and padding over the site. Cast a concrete slab in the bottom of the hole, on top of the padding. Build a brick wall on the slab. The liner runs up the outside of the wall; pack sand between the sandwich and the sides of the hole. Top with hardpan, sand and the paving.

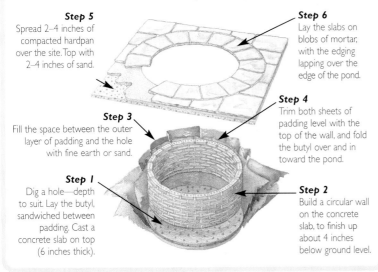

Step 5
Spread 2–4 inches of compacted hardpan over the site. Top with 2–4 inches of sand.

Step 3
Fill the space between the outer layer of padding and the hole with fine earth or sand.

Step 1
Dig a hole—depth to suit. Lay the butyl, sandwiched between padding. Cast a concrete slab on top (6 inches thick).

Step 6
Lay the slabs on blobs of mortar, with the edging lapping over the edge of the pond.

Step 4
Trim both sheets of padding level with the top of the wall, and fold the butyl over and in toward the pond.

Step 2
Build a circular wall on the concrete slab, to finish up about 4 inches below ground level.

FOUNTAINS, PUMPS, AND FILTERS

If you want a fountain in the pond, you will need to fit a pump. If you are going to have a formal pond with a few plants and fish, you will need a pump and filter. These have to be planned at an early stage, so that water pipes and power cables can be hidden from view.

For example, the sunken pond opposite would need two pipes (one for water and the other to protect the power cable) running from the inside of the pond, through the bottom of the wall, up between the outside of the wall and the padding, over the top of the wall, and under the patio paving. All you will see is the pump and filter at the bottom of the pond.

For a raised pond, the best you can do is to disguise the piping. The pump sits in the bottom of the pond, the water pipe and the cable run up the inside of the pond and over the top edge, where you discreetly try to hide them under the coping, pebbles, or perhaps a well placed plant.

Small water features

Can I have a feature with moving water on my patio?

A small water feature can transform a patio from a mere place to park a chair into a haven where you can enjoy the delightful sounds of water trickling, bubbling, or gushing. There are lots of small, self-contained water features that do not involve building a pond; some do not even require the effort of digging a hole. Container ponds bring all the charms of a full-size pond, with a lot less effort. Visit a water garden center to look at all the possibilities on offer.

OPTIONS FOR SMALL WATER FEATURES

Container ponds

↗ A container pond can be made in anything from a large, ceramic pot to a wooden half-barrel. Just fill it with water, and add a few aquatic plants such as hornwort or irises. Another idea is to group a collection of containers, each of which is planted with different species.

Bubble fountains

↗ Bubble fountains consist of a fountainhead and a pump in a sump (or reservoir), which is set above or below ground. This is covered by your choice of feature, such as a millstone or pebbles. The pump pushes the water up through the fountainhead to run over the display before seeping back into the sump. This is an attractive, low-cost option.

Wall mask waterspout

↗ A wall mask waterspout gushes water into a reservoir pool at the base. A pump is placed in the reservoir, and connected to a delivery pipe that runs up the back of the wall and through the mask. To make life easier, an existing wall is preferable.

A ready-made water feature, which just needs to be filled with water and plugged in. It is attractive and safe, and children will love it. Together with many similar designs, it is available at a reasonable cost.

Container ponds

A container pond is no more than a container that holds water, so there are many suitable candidates. Here are some ideas, but you can also use many unusual items creatively.

Oak half-barrel ~ Wooden half-barrels make attractive containers. Soak them in water until the staves swell up and the barrel becomes watertight. The genuine article is preferable to reproductions.

Glazed ceramic pots ~ It is possible to buy ceramic pots in all shapes and sizes. Get the biggest that you can find. Drainage holes will have to be plugged with corks.

Galvanized water tank ~ Old galvanized house water supply tanks make capacious container ponds. They take on a special charm when full of water and an interesting range of plants.

Lead tank ~ These are quite difficult to find, but look imposing. Try searching in junkyards and at architectural salvage companies.

Galvanized buckets and baths ~ Galvanized buckets, bathtubs, troughs, watering cans, and cattle feeders look great—the bigger and older the better.

This old stone trough has great character and makes a stunning container pond.

HOW TO BUILD A BUBBLING URN FEATURE

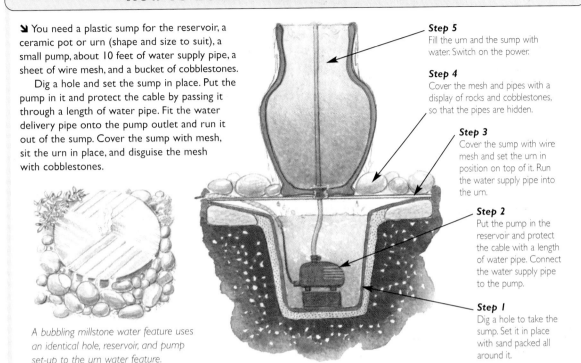

↘ You need a plastic sump for the reservoir, a ceramic pot or urn (shape and size to suit), a small pump, about 10 feet of water supply pipe, a sheet of wire mesh, and a bucket of cobblestones.

Dig a hole and set the sump in place. Put the pump in it and protect the cable by passing it through a length of water pipe. Fit the water delivery pipe onto the pump outlet and run it out of the sump. Cover the sump with mesh, sit the urn in place, and disguise the mesh with cobblestones.

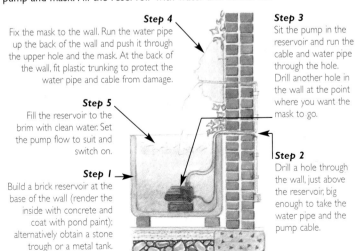

A bubbling millstone water feature uses an identical hole, reservoir, and pump set-up to the urn water feature.

Step 5
Fill the urn and the sump with water. Switch on the power.

Step 4
Cover the mesh and pipes with a display of rocks and cobblestones, so that the pipes are hidden.

Step 3
Cover the sump with wire mesh and set the urn in position on top of it. Run the water supply pipe into the urn.

Step 2
Put the pump in the reservoir and protect the cable with a length of water pipe. Connect the water supply pipe to the pump.

Step 1
Dig a hole to take the sump. Set it in place with sand packed all around it.

HOW TO BUILD A WALL MASK WATERSPOUT

If you have an existing patio with a concrete footing and a brick wall at one side, you can have a wall mask waterspout. Build a brick reservoir to match the wall (or use a ready-made trough or tank). Drill a hole through the wall, just above the brim of the reservoir, for the water pipe and the power cable. Drill a second hole where the mask is to hang. Sit the pump in the reservoir, and run the cable through the wall. Connect the ends of the water pipe to the pump and mask. Fill the reservoir with water and switch on.

Step 4
Fix the mask to the wall. Run the water pipe up the back of the wall and push it through the upper hole and the mask. At the back of the wall, fit plastic trunking to protect the water pipe and cable from damage.

Step 5
Fill the reservoir to the brim with clean water. Set the pump flow to suit and switch on.

Step 1
Build a brick reservoir at the base of the wall (render the inside with concrete and coat with pond paint); alternatively obtain a stone trough or a metal tank.

Step 3
Sit the pump in the reservoir and run the cable and water pipe through the hole. Drill another hole in the wall at the point where you want the mask to go.

Step 2
Drill a hole through the wall, just above the reservoir, big enough to take the water pipe and the pump cable.

PUMP POWER

The greater the head height (vertical distance from water surface to fountainhead) and spray height, the higher the flow rate needed. To calculate a pump's flow rate, time how long it takes to fill a container of known capacity—if it takes ten minutes to fill 50 gallons, the flow rate is 300 gallons per hour.

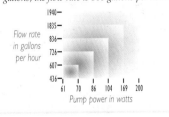

Flow rate in gallons per hour

| 1940— |
| 1835— |
| 836— |
| 726— |
| 607— |
| 436— |

61 70 86 104 169 200
Pump power in watts

ELECTRICITY AND SAFETY

- *Always fit a circuit interrupter (GFCI) between the pump and the power supply, to protect yourself from electric shock.*

- *Make sure that all cables and outlets are designed for outside use.*

- *It is good practice to avoid putting your hands in the water when the power is on, even if there is a GFCI.*

Barbecues

Is it safe to have a barbecue on a patio?

Patios and barbecues make perfect partners. There is something really enjoyable about eating outdoors— what could be better, on a warm summer's evening, than to light the barbecue, cook a meal, and then sit back and relax on the patio. If you wish, you can build in a barbecue as a permanent feature.

BARBECUE OPTIONS

Built-in barbecue

↗ *A built-in brick barbecue makes an attractive patio feature. Consider carefully where you want it sited.*

Charcoal barbecues

↗ *There is something special about lighting and using a charcoal barbecue—it imparts a back-to-nature feel to cooking.*

Gas barbecue

↗ *If you would prefer to avoid the rituals of using a charcoal barbecue, a gas barbecue is a problem-free alternative.*

Disposable barbecue

↗ *A disposable barbecue is a great idea when there isn't room for a permanent set-up. It also avoids the need to buy charcoal.*

BEST POSITION

If you are planning to build a barbecue on the patio, think carefully about where to put it. Take into account safety aspects in relation to items such as decking and shades. Assess the distance from the proposed barbecue to the table for suitability. Consider the direction of prevailing winds. Will the site will upset your neighbors?

When you have chosen a promising site, have a trial run by setting up a table to represent the barbecue. See what it feels like walking backward and forward from the "barbecue" to where you will be sitting. If you need a power source, consider how you are going to safely route the cable.

WINTER STORAGE

Portable charcoal, gas and electric barbecues, and the trays and grills of brick barbecues, need to be stored away in winter, ideally in a dry and well ventilated shed or garage.

Clean trays and grills before packing them away, and store gas bottles, fuel and charcoal as recommended by the manufacturer. Clean all barbecue tools before putting them away.

HOW TO BUILD A BRICK BARBECUE

Search out a basic barbecue complete with a charcoal tray, cooking grill, and fixings—or have a welder make one up to your own design. You also need a bag of mortar mix, a carpenter's level, a set square, a tape measure, a small trowel, a plastic bucket, and a piece of board about 1 yard square. Use a piece of chalk to mark out your chosen site. Mix the mortar on the board as directed, and dampen the bricks with water.

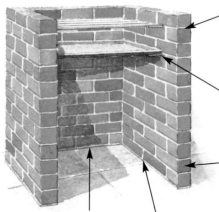

Step 5
When the mortar has partially set, use a trowel to tidy up the mortar and also to rake a little mortar from all the joints.

Step 4
Continue until you reach the recommended height. Push the metal support strips into the mortar joints.

Step 3
Spread mortar on the first course of bricks and bed the second course of dampened bricks in place.

Step 1
Brush the site clear of debris. Do a trial placing of the first and second courses of bricks, so you know what goes where.

Step 2
Dampen the bricks, spread mortar and bed the first course in place. Use a carpenter's level to test for vertical and horizontal alignment.

Lighting and heating

The sun may have gone down, but that doesn't mean you have to abandon the patio and go indoors. It is possible to enjoy your patio until late at night, and it can take on a new persona as a romantic or dramatic venue for entertaining. There are all kinds of lights available, from electric to gas, or those based on candles. If it is late in the season and the air is getting chilly, there are wood and charcoal burners, or gas heaters, to make the patio comfortable.

How do I get maximum use out of my patio?

Planning lighting and heating for a new patio

Getting professional advice ~ If you are building a new patio from scratch and you know that you will want electric lighting and heating, plan out the position of the items and build ducting, outlets and supports into the design. Unless you are very confident about your proficiency, this is one of those times when it is best to bring in a professional to help, advise, and do the tricky bits.

LIGHTING OPTIONS

General lighting ~ Available lighting ranges from genuine antique street lights to subtle uplighters and downlighters, and lights that illuminate the whole patio. Avoid lights that shine into your eyes. Low-voltage lights are a quick and easy option.

Table lighting ~ Table lights are designed to cast light on the eating area. Small candle lanterns are easy on the eyes and great for setting a mood.

Lighting for effect ~ Lights can add interest and excitement to a patio. Try party lights, Christmas lights, Chinese lanterns, or coach lights. Spotlights can be used to highlight plants or a water feature.

A modern globe light

A pretty candle lantern

Patio heaters

Gas and electric heaters are certainly instant and efficient (within a radius of a couple of yards), but nothing is quite so dynamic as a traditional woodburning stove with a chimney. The drawback is that it can be difficult to light, smoky, and needs watching. On the plus side, a stove makes an exciting addition.

General lighting

General lighting for the patio is much the same as general lighting in the home—it consists of straightforward overhead or wall lights that illuminate a space.

You need one or more of these no-nonsense lights around the patio area. Small wall lights are a good option—they are relatively inexpensive and easy to install. If your patio is remote from the house and without walls, use standard lights or tree lights.

Lighting for effect

General lights are ideal for illuminating a whole area, but you need smaller lights in order to create a mood or effect. There are lots of options. You can have strings of little colored lights, lanterns, lights half-buried in the ground, high-tech solar lights, spirit torches that are spiked in the ground, scented candles, and so on.

There are two safety issues to take into account—children and candles are a bad mix, and strong flashing lights are not good for people who are partially sighted or who suffer from migraines.

Table lighting

If you are planning an after-dark dinner party, the table needs to be lit in some way. There are many electric lights to choose from, but the drawback of a power cable is that it is unsightly and presents a potential trip hazard. It is much better to deck your table with an assortment of lanterns, or tea lights in colored glass jars—the flickering shadows they create look wonderful.

Protect yourself by using a circuit breaker

For safety's sake, all garden electrics need to be fitted with a GFCI (Ground Fault Circuit Interrupter), commonly known as a safety cut-out. This inexpensive and completely necessary device ensures that the power is instantly cut off if the cable is damaged by accident.

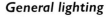
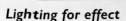

Index